A British MP's tryst with Parleela in Parliament

An Anglo-Indian Encounter

Parleela in Parliament, creative nonfiction, is part of The Englandia Quartet comprising of *Lalluva goes to London*, *Inside Curry Palace of London* and *The Twain.*

factionbooks@gmail.com

CONTENTS

f&f

facts n' fiction

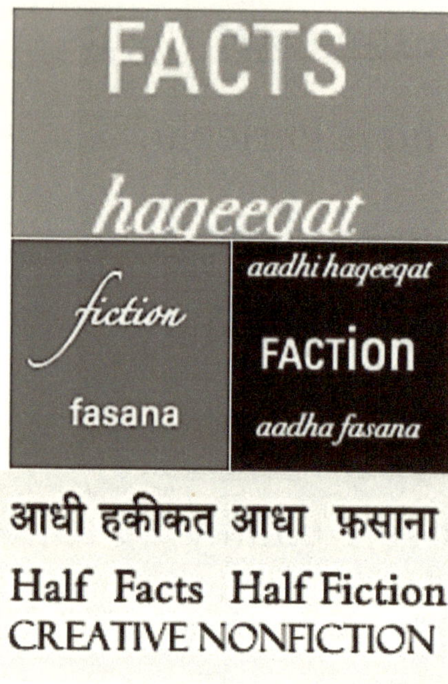

Introduction

British imperial power and the Indian woman had an intense intercourse influenced by the gender equations in Victorian Britain and the penchant for masculine adventures abroad.

The colony was seen as a female form. The Indian woman was considered to be a seductive, weak but dangerous piece of strange territory to be kept under control.

The sexual allure of the alien continues in post-imperial Britain. The intersection of gender and race makes cross-cultural affairs colourful. The tabloids go wild if a two-timing English Member of Parliament is found entangled with a nonwhite female.

Parliament boasts of a liberal atmosphere in which married male MPs flirt with female secretaries and researchers. Women are groped or addressed by pet names such as "sugar tits". Some MPs go beyond flirting but the victims rarely break their silence. If an odd one dares to speak out long after the incident, her complaint gets noted only by the tabloids.

No serious attempt is made to reform Westminster's culture. An extra-marital affair never costs a political career. An erring MP is defended by the Prime Minister. Every sex scandal is followed by a routine statement that "the public expect MPs to conduct themselves to the highest possible standards".

In reality, the voters like their MPs behaving badly. They know that the MPs, like them, are human. They live away from their wives and work late into the night.

Rt. Hon. Dick Carnall MP is a major player in the political theatre of Westminster. He feels morally superior since he never fudged his expense account, never took cash for questions, never struck a fellow MP in the Parliament bar, and was never found lying on the footpath late at night. He managed to keep himself out of the list of MPs involved in what the feminists call sexual misconduct.

Carnall discreetly carries on with his beautiful research assistant of Indian origin. To the delight of her boss, Parleela, the Brit-Indian, does more than research. As an argumentative female, she feels good discussing Love and Lust with a powerful man. She explores her own heart; Carnall explores her body.

CHAPTER ONE

Westminster Nights
MP's OFFICE

DICK CARNALL: Come, come, my pretty assistant. Assist me. Come.

PARLEELA: I am here.

DICK CARNALL: Parleela, my Parliamentary perk. Parleela, my playful pet. Parleela, my private pleasure. Parleela, my past, my present.

PARLEELA: And future?

DICK CARNALL: The future lies in future. *One-two-three-four-five-six-seven, all good men go to heaven!*

PARLEELA: I get the scent of a drunken man.

DICK CARNALL: I get the scent of a desirable woman.

PARLEELA: Please go and splash water on your face.

DICK CARNALL: I had one for the road and one for thee.

PARLEELA: The bell is chiming. It's three.

DICK CARNALL: Here we are just you and me.

PARLEELA: Drink hard and you won't be the Prime Minister.

DICK CARNALL: A drunken Dick is better than a sober Prick.

PARLEELA: Bush turned a teetotaler to become the President.

DICK CARNALL: We are civilised, not Americans.

PARLEELA: Of course! Churchill ran the country in a state he would not have been allowed to run a car!

DICK CARNALL: Water makes a wimp! Liquor is quicker!

PARLEELA: Drink provokes desire but takes away performance!

DICK CARNALL: I drink and perform. Fill my cup. Come ride on me! Let the journey begin!

PARLEELA: Beginning is fine but where do we end?

DICK CARNALL: In our beginning is our end!

PARLEELA: Words. Words. Words. Don't fob me off with words. The heating switched off at midnight. Bankrupt Britain! I'm cold.

DICK CARNALL: Come, I heat you up!

PARLEELA: I'm no English heroine "in heat like a bride in a bath..."

DICK CARNALL: Tom Stoppard! Let's enact a play. This sofa is our stage.

PARLEELA: The Palace of Westminster was built as a theatre of state.

DICK CARNALL: Now it is a theatre of love.

PARLEELA: The Rt. Hon. MP confuses lawmaking with lovemaking.

DICK CARNALL: Lovemaking lubricates the wheels of democracy.

PARLEELA: Democratisation of love! Westminster Palace promotes it.

DICK CARNALL: It gives us the freedom to love.

PARLEELA: You call it love. The media calls it sleaze.

DICK CARNALL: They insert words such as groping and sexual misconduct into love stories. The media has no empathy for the MPs who lead a lonely life in London.

PARLEELA: The MPs are not special. All Britons are afflicted with loneliness. The Prime Minister had to appoint a Minister for Loneliness!

DICK CARNALL: I will give you that portfolio. You are a perfect antidote for my loneliness!

PARLEELA: Can a sex pest of Westminster ever be the Prime Minister?

DICK CARNALL: I'm not among the 36 Tory MPs featured in the "Spreadsheet of Shame" circulated by a bloody secret group.

PARLEELA: How did you manage to evade police investigation!

DICK CARNALL: Because I'm a man of sterling character!

PARLEELA: Wait till the #MeToo brigade catches you!

DICK CARNALL: The #MeToo brigade has turned up like worms in the uncivilised US. Our women are imitating their American sisters and narrating lurid events that took place years ago. Only French women understand men. They appreciate the art of seduction! They disapprove of what their American sisters are doing.

PARLEELA: Justice may be delayed; it would not be denied!

DICK CARNALL: False memory! The US media is using it to sell sensation. We in Britain never went through a trial by media on this scale.

PARLEELA: Even the British media uncovered Westminster's sex scandals. A Tory woman MP turned novelist and revealed it all.

DICK CARNALL: The one with red shoes and attractive ankles.

PARLEELA: She will expose you in her next novel *Legislating Love*!

DICK CARNALL: The Prime Minister is having an affair with her.

PARLEELA: This Prime Minister doesn't look that sort.

DICK CARNALL: What do you mean that sort?

PARLEELA: Not colourful.

DICK CARNALL: He is colourful inside!

PARLEELA: He wears a grey suit and tucks his shirt into his underwear.

DICK CARNALL: What he looks like and what he does are different.

PARLEELA: You are like him!

DICK CARNALL: We are not an odd couple! This very moment, most of my colleagues are somewhat similarly engaged.

PARLEELA: In this building?

DICK CARNALL: In this historic building!

PARLEELA: Under its Gothic heights!

DICK CARNALL: Watched over by Barry and Pugin!

PARLEELA: By statues and painted figures!

DICK CARNALL: By peers and prelates.

PARLEELA: Tudor faces and Arthurian frescos.

DICK CARNALL: Armorial bearings and heraldic devices.

PARLEELA: Light filtering through stained glass.

DICK CARNALL: Magnificent! Like an Oriental pleasure dome.

PARLEELA: Pleasure den!

DICK CARNALL: An English Taj Mahal!

PARLEELA: A monument to whose love?

DICK CARNALL: My love for you!

PARLEELA: This Cathedral of Democracy has been turned into a Temple of Mammon. Once these walls resounded to the oratory of Churchill, to Latin quotations, Shakespearean lines, Burkian logic and Greek rhetoric.

DICK CARNALL: We are proud of our glorious past!

PARLEELA: Talk of the seedy present! This crumbling Palace of Westminster symbolises the depraved political culture.

DICK CARNALL: You read too much of *The Guardian*!

PARLEELA: Millions of pounds of public money will be wasted on renovating this temple of democracy that has lost its soul.

DICK CARNALL: I don't like the idea of moving into a modern structure for a few years. We feel secure in this castle. Safe from public scrutiny, from the prying eyes. Imagine you and me having this conversation in a glass house. That will destroy the love lives of MPs.

PARLEELA: Uses of privacy!

DICK CARNALL: This building gives us complete privacy. A Tory lawmaker is making a baby right now in his office!

PARLEELA: That baby one day will be on the front page of the *Sun*!

DICK CARNALL: Another MP is in the arms of a Polish researcher.

PARLEELA: That innocent Polish girl will speak out one day through #MeToo!

DICK CARNALL: Lord Dandelion is lying inert over a divorced West Indian.

PARLEELA: Tina Brown wrote about an ageing Lord whose secretary is "a pretty, silent blonde girl with whom he enjoys recreational humiliation." How do the doddering old peers do it?

DICK CARNALL: You should hear them talking!

PARLEELA: What do they say?

DICK CARNALL: They fantasise. A Tory Minister was obsessed with Margaret Thatcher's foot. A Tory Lord goes gaga about a woman MP's legs. Another one is obsessed with a lesbian journalist. James desires to "roger" a woman minister. He declares his intention to his friends.

PARLEELA: I hear his rival calling every woman MP 'Betty'.

DICK CARNALL: One Rt. Hon. Member is seen grasping imaginary breasts!

PARLEELA: The situation has got out of hands. Parliament's toilets are in the news! Shared combs and brushes removed from the cloakrooms for fear of head lice and HIV infection!

Dick Carnall: One minister fearful of HIV used to send his secretary to buy sex toys for him!

Parleela: The Honourable Members who share research assistants may not fear HIV but aren't they afraid of the Prime Minister?

Dick Carnall: The Prime Minister will stand by us. He will tell the people that our private lives do not affect the conduct of our public duties.

Parleela: Were you cautious when a Prime Minister launched his Back-to-Basics campaign? Were you made to give up your extra-legislative activity with my predecessors?

Dick Carnall: It made no difference.

Parleela: Disgraceful! This great institution has lost its reputation!

Dick Carnall: Why blame the MPs? Did you not see *The Financial Times* the other day? Did you not read what the City's leaders did to the women recruited for their prestigious event one night?

Parleela: It is said that the Tory MPs are starved of sex and the Labour MPs want money. I see them all wanting more of everything!

Dick Carnall: I want more of you!

PARLEELA: The Prime Minister famous for his Westminster Clean-up Campaign was found to have been involved in an extra-marital affair!

DICK CARNALL: A former MP said he saw things happening but he himself was not involved since his family lived in London!

PARLEELA: You expect public sympathy for those MPs whose families do not live in London!

DICK CARNALL: Of course!

PARLEELA: The public will not keep quiet now that the sex pests of Westminster are hitting the headlines every day!

DICK CARNALL: The media has gone mad!

PARLEELA: A couple of noble souls have confessed to sexual misconduct and paid a token price.

DICK CARNALL: Once the political storm subsides, they will return. It will be business as usual.

PARLEELA: The accused MPs are making the whole nation queasy! This is what the commentators are saying.

DICK CARNALL: Let them say what they say! There is no such thing as "unwanted sexual behaviour". The saner voices call it a witch-hunt!

PARLEELA: Your "saner voices" warn the whistle-blowing women against killing romance. They say men will stop flirting out of fear.

DICK CARNALL: How will we function if the Bar hours or the number of our guests are restricted?

PARLEELA: How will you function if a woman journalist hesitates to dine with you?

DICK CARNALL: This wave of Puritanism, this sexual counter-revolution will fizzle out.

PARLEELA: You mean human nature will reassert itself.

DICK CARNALL: Human behaviour cannot be changed. There will be a backlash. The swinging sixties will return.

PARLEELA: We won't be there then!

DICK CARNALL: Let's swing here and now.

PARLEELA: You will not desist despite the protests by the feminists?

DICK CARNALL: Of course not! Let the man-haters do their worst!

PARLEELA: You are not scared of the #MeToo campaign. So many women victims are recalling what men did to them.

DICK CARNALL: You would never do that, not tomorrow, not the day after! I feel safe with you!

PARLEELA: Someone else may harm you! You ought to worry about your political career.

DICK CARNALL: No one can touch me. The Government will be destabilised if they try to harm me.

PARLEELA: I can't say about me but the Government will survive without you!

DICK CARNALL: My character is flawless! What can they say against me? I do nothing that Westminster's newly formed moral police has cautioned the MPs against. Do I touch your knee?

PARLEELA: You skip my knees and aim higher!

DICK CARNALL: Do I slap your bum? Do I cup? Do I grope? Do I fondle?

PARLEELA: You come to the point straightaway!

DICK CARNALL: Is that sexual harassment?

PARLEELA: No. Just "good humoured high jinks", as an accused MP said.

DICK CARNALL: They cannot charge me with coercion or exploitation. Did I ever promise to help you with your career?

PARLEELA: Never.

DICK CARNALL: Nothing non-consensual in our case!

PARLEELA: Semi-consensual!

DICK CARNALL: We can go on without fear!

PARLEELA: One day a woman Prime Minister will clean up Westminster. If she succeeds, she would have saved democracy.

DICK CARNALL: A woman Prime Minister increases lust.

PARLEELA: Of course, women Prime Ministers come and go.

DICK CARNALL: You and I go on forever!

PARLEELA: In the present situation, why don't you cancel our nightly work schedule for some days?

DICK CARNALL: Don't you worry. This fit of moral panic will not last.

PARLEELA: Some of your quotes may come to haunt you. Stop claiming that you are morally engaged.

DICK CARNALL: That must be said in public.

PARLEELA: While doing things in private.

DICK CARNALL: The political imperative, my love!

PARLEELA: What about the moral imperative?

DICK CARNALL: Without these affairs, Britain will have no politics.

PARLEELA: Without touching and groping, petting, and kissing, the party conferences will be deserted!

DICK CARNALL: What else is there in this Palace of Westminster? Take away sex and who would like to be an MP?

PARLEELA: The US uses sex for recruiting sportsmen!

DICK CARNALL: We use it for a higher purpose. Aren't you proud of your contribution to democracy?

PARLEELA: I'm proud of being useful to you!

DICK CARNALL: Be alert. Some forces are ranged against us. They alleged that some MPs were taking money for asking questions! They charged some MPs with falsification of accounts. They questioned our expenses to sabotage Parliament's functioning.

PARLEELA: So mean! They disapproved of the MPs claiming one pound for cleaning gloves, 2.49 pounds for hand towels and 9.78 pounds for a washing-up bowl!

DICK CARNALL: One MP was criticised for buying a clock for his office with public money!

PARLEELA: Some MPs had to sleep on office floors to reduce their expense claims!

DICK CARNALL: One more bureaucratic body IPSA, the Independent Parliamentary Standards Authority, was established.

PARLEELA: The MPs complained that they were being "ensnared in a vice-like grip designed to bring them into disrepute".

DICK CARNALL: A conspiracy to destroy democracy in Britain by ruining the financial and sex lives of MPs!

PARLEELA: Let's move from the political to the personal. Today I ask you who am I to you?

DICK CARNALL: Time will tell.

PARLEELA: Hurry up, it is time!

DICK CARNALL: I am ready. Feel me.

PARLEELA: Where?

DICK CARNALL: Here, here, and here, as a famous British politician once said!

PARLEELA: He got banished from politics for his anti-immigrant rhetoric. And he had pointed only towards his heart.

DICK CARNALL: My heart is differently located!

PARLEELA: Love means living together!

DICK CARNALL: We live together for precious moments!

PARLEELA: Fudge, fudge, fudge, that's all you do. Love must have a map.

DICK CARNALL: Lady, shall I lie in your lap?

PARLEELA: You are merry my Lord!

DICK CARNALL: You are far, my Lady!

PARLEELA: What use is being near? You'll lie in my lap and take a nap. Like *The Lullaby* lover.

DICK CARNALL: You called me lover! I'm your lover!

PARLEELA: Keep fantasising!

DICK CARNALL: You are lovely! Dark face, deep eyes, brown arms. White & brown. We are perfect partners.

PARLEELA: There you go about my colour!

DICK CARNALL: Your hair is black!

PARLEELA: My hair was not made black to entice you. I was not coloured to excite you.

DICK CARNALL: I am a sucker for black hair. Yeats was for yellow hair.

PARLEELA: I am no white man's artefact.

DICK CARNALL: You are Indian sunshine!

PARLEELA: My body is not the text of empire.

DICK CARNALL: You are my cup of Indian tea.

PARLEELA: Your plate of cross-cultural curry!

DICK CARNALL: The dusky daughter of Hindostan!

PARLEELA: Locating me by my skin!

DICK CARNALL: Positioning you by your scent! Seeking you by your heat! I'm a missile heading for the target!

PARLEELA: You misread my warmth! Look behind my dark eyes!

DICK CARNALL: You quiver. I wrap you in an intercultural embrace!

PARLEELA: Embrace between a man and woman is carnal.

DICK CARNALL: Let's pretend to be men then.

PARLEELA: Pigment and climate make us incompatible. You're from the West, I'm from the East. You are for action. I'm for thought.

DICK CARNALL: We are plug and socket!

PARLEELA: Sky and rocket!

DICK CARNALL: Let's go to India. Sultry rhymes with adultery. Lust rhymes with dust. There was beauty in the Empire.

PARLEELA: An imperial illusion!

DICK CARNALL: An imperial allusion!

PARLEELA: A colonial fallacy!

DICK CARNALL: Metaphors of possession and ravishment!

PARLEELA: Binarism.

DICK CARNALL: We shall be one tonight.

PARLEELA: The twain shall never meet!

DICK CARNALL: I love Indian. I do Indian.

PARLEELA: I do English!

DICK CARNALL: We overwrite our past. A palimpsest on palimpsest!

PARLEELA: That's the nature of Truth.

DICK CARNALL: Let's give and take.

PARLEELA: That's not your tradition.

DICK CARNALL: Our relationship was not one-sided. We shared hopes, desires, and anxieties. Aziz was no "little Indian".

PARLEELA: I am no promise. I'm not Forster's India.

DICK CARNALL: I'm no Forster. I'm normal.

PARLEELA: Love between men is the bulwark of English culture!

DICK CARNALL: Look who's stereotyping now!

PARLEELA: You fetishise me.

DICK CARNALL: You seduce me.

PARLEELA: You are seduced by my otherness.

DICK CARNALL: I am not othering you. Come and be one! Let me show you!

PARLEELA: *Show Me* is what I said yesterday. *Do Me* is what I sing today.

DICK CARNALL: I'm ready to do. I'm a plumber. British women want to do the plumber. "The plumber knows what he's doing", says David Hare.

PARLEELA: You are unipolar.

DICK CARNALL: You are bipolar. The twin Oriental domes.

PARLEELA: The music of the spheres!

DICK CARNALL: Let's play a costume drama!

PARLEELA: All play and no work will make you a jerk!

DICK CARNALL: We are old friends.

PARLEELA: Modern partners.

DICK CARNALL: Engaged in a relationship!

PARLEELA: Commanded by your monarch?

DICK CARNALL: Yes. Tonight, ParlDarl and Dick Carnall drink to the Anglo-Indian partnership.

PARLEELA: A limited partnership?

DICK CARNALL: Limited by my wife.

PARLEELA: Doesn't your wife know you?

DICK CARNALL: She knows what we do.

PARLEELA: Really! I must fear her then!

DICK CARNALL: My wife reads the debates and she reads my speeches.

PARLEELA: Does she not read reports of the cannabis found in Parliamentary toilets? Does she not read about the MPs apologising for sexual misconduct? What about the explosive novels *A Parliamentary Affair* and *Memoirs of Merlin*?

DICK CARNALL: She is a Tory wife! She reads, hears, and sees but come the elections, she stands by me before the cameras.

PARLEELA: Still, you must be careful.

DICK CARNALL: Even the Home Secretary couldn't be too careful. You saw that!

PARLEELA: Does your wife know you are with me at this hour of the night?

DICK CARNALL: That cow doesn't know.

PARLEELA: You call your woman a cow!

DICK CARNALL: An Indian artist painted a composite of woman and cow. *Kamdhenu*!

PARLEELA: One of Margaret Thatcher's ministers called her cow behind her back!

DICK CARNALL: That junior Trade Minister didn't know a thing about women!

PARLEELA: Francois Mitterrand said Mrs Thatcher had the eyes of Caligula but the mouth of

Marilyn Monroe. He didn't say which part interested him more.

DICK CARNALL: Mitterrand liked every part of the woman.

PARLEELA: Maggie impressed Gorbachev and won the cold war!

DICK CARNALL: We all loved the stern mistress!

PARLEELA: The whip-wielding mistress could not tame love.

DICK CARNALL: The Thatcher years saw no decline in lovemaking!

PARLEELA: The Iron Lady herself never fell in love.

DICK CARNALL: Maggie inspired lust.

PARLEELA: Admiration, hatred, and anger.

DICK CARNALL: But never love.

PARLEELA: She put a price to everything and yet free love flourished in her reign!

DICK CARNALL: She said there is no such thing as society.

PARLEELA: She stood for a free world and free trade, not for free love.

DICK CARNALL: Maggie didn't understand. If you free the market, love too gets freed. Free market undermines established patterns of belief and behaviour.

PARLEELA: Free love leads to free market.

DICK CARNALL: Let's not cheapen free love.

PARLEELA: You talk like Tom Stoppard, the word lover!

DICK CARNALL: Indulges in infinite foreplay.

PARLEELA: Maggie did inspire lust. Her minister Alan Clark couldn't take his eyes off her. In his Dairies, he confessed his feelings "of the other kind" for his Prime Minister. It was not love because that womanising MP, serial philanderer, upper-class hooligan, was not capable of loving!

DICK CARNALL: The Edwardian bounder is remembered as a national hero.

PARLEELA: A BBC documentary paid rich tributes to him. Posthumously, Alan Clark delivered a record audience to BBC TV.

DICK CARNALL: The BBC hit a gold mine because Alan had carried on simultaneously with a married mother and her two daughters. He called the female trio "The Coven"!

PARLEELA: Alan's wife knew all about his affairs.

DICK CARNALL: Of course! She found him "such fun"! She helped him carry on. She even cooperated in the making of the documentary on Alan's philandering. Alan had an understanding wife.

PARLEELA: Tory wives are model wives.

DICK CARNALL: That's why we are morally engaged!

PARLEELA: I must thank your wife!

CHAPTER TWO

Who is Parleela?
MP's OFFICE

DICK CARNALL: Refill my glass. Come nearer.

PARLEELA: You stink!

DICK CARNALL: You took my breath test. Take my lust test.

PARLEELA: Your lust has passed all tests!

DICK CARNALL: I need a fresh certificate!

PARLEELA: Don't you try to be Alan Clark. I admired him.

DICK CARNALL: He had a way with women.

PARLEELA: A perfect Etonian!

DICK CARNALL: Eton produced leaders in every field—philosophy to physics, politics to philandering.

PARLEELA: Gunrunners. Wife-runners. The number of wives who ran away with Etonians!

DICK CARNALL: Our wars were won on the playing fields of Harrow and Eton.

PARLEELA: They groomed coup-plotters to take over every small oil and diamond-producing state.

DICK CARNALL: I am ready to take you over.

PARLEELA: Stop the chatter. How do you want me?

DICK CARNALL: I want you rare, I want you well done. I want you in the morning. I want you in the evening. I want you in summer. But most of all, I want you in winter.

PARLEELA: I meant why did you want me tonight?

DICK CARNALL: For urgent business!

PARLEELA: Let's get down to it then. No hanky-panky tonight.

DICK CARNALL: Come. With your touch, I remake myself. Pour me more.

PARLEELA: Here you are!

DICK CARNALL: To us!

PARLEELA: To us!

(Glasses tinkle)

DICK CARNALL: Now tell me, will you? Will you?

PARLEELA: Yes, I say yes, I will, yes.

DICK CARNALL: Of my pleasure you are the source.

PARLEELA: Don't you try to use force!

DICK CARNALL: You are my great resource.

PARLEELA: All that is fine. What is my official assignment?

DICK CARNALL: The PM wants a brief on the Indian Prime Minister visiting Britain. He is looking for skeletons in Mr Lalluva's cupboard.

PARLEELA: The PM normally wants dope on his rivals in the party. Why is he bothered about a foreign leader?

DICK CARNALL: Information is power. The US Republicans had asked John Major to share the file on Bill Clinton's Oxford year as a Rhodes Scholar. The PM wants to know about Mr Lalluva.

PARLEELA: But why?

DICK CARNALL: Mr Lalluva represents the biggest arms market.

PARLEELA: Are some sensitive negotiations on with India?

DICK CARNALL: The PM wants to avoid embarrassment during the state visit. Suppose the Indian Prime Minister turns up with a woman masquerading as his spouse. An African leader brought along his seventh wife pregnant with her chauffeur's child. The British monarch had to greet that woman in the palace!

PARLEELA: Is the Indian Prime Minister a suspect?

DICK CARNALL: Our young singer *folly* was closeted with the Indian Prime Minister in his office for an extended one-to-one session. Our High Commissioner was unable to confirm the rumours floating in New Delhi.

PARLEELA: *folly* has nothing in common with the rustic Mr Lalluva.

DICK CARNALL: *folly* went to India in search of spirituality. She said she was there to discover herself. Such seekers can do anything. Our women have gone out of control.

PARLEELA: Some of them go to Africa to pay tributes to the African male.

DICK CARNALL: An English woman went to India and married an illiterate villager who drives a taxi!

PARLEELA: A British armament company paid for folly's India trip. Its liaison agent in New Delhi fixed her appointment with the Indian Prime Minister! I will check for details with my sources in the Indian High Commission.

DICK CARNALL: The Prime Minister is impressed by your research! I am impressed by the researcher!

PARLEELA: Shall we come to the business of the night.

DICK CARNALL: This is my nightly business. Give me more!

(Glasses tinkle)

PARLEELA: Mr Lalluva is unmarried.

DICK CARNALL: Why is Mr Lalluva unmarried? Therein lies a tale! He may have a woman hidden in his village. Or did he abandon the child bride he married as a young boy! Any hanky-panky in his life?

PARLEELA: More hanky-panky goes on in this Palace of Westminster than in New Delhi.

DICK CARNALL: We conduct propah parliamentary affairs.

PARLEELA: With you as the minister in charge!

DICK CARNALL: This building has the Royal Robing Room. My room is the Disrobing Room.

PARLEELA: Aren't we supposed to work?

DICK CARNALL: You are my work. I do you.

PARLEELA: You will do me in. Let's work. Work is worship.

DICK CARNALL: You want to worship me? Let's do it in a church!

PARLEELA: Graham Greene's influence!

DICK CARNALL: He holds no patent on the process.

PARLEELA: Seduction in cathedral is less sinful than a murder!

DICK CARNALL: There is no sex without nuns and no redemption without wine. I read it somewhere.

PARLEELA: If you pray, you will be rewarded with virgins in paradise.

DICK CARNALL: My paradise is just inches away! I am ready to enter!

PARLEELA: You know what you want. I don't know whether I ache with unassuaged desire or fear diminution of passion.

DICK CARNALL: I will not let it diminish!

PARLEELA: Who am I? What do I do? What shall I be? Should I be a poet's dream or a gunner's sight?

DICK CARNALL: Be mine!

PARLEELA: A musician's muse, a painter's plaything, a playwright's character, a director's heroine! I bubble with creative energy. I want to be a writer.

DICK CARNALL: Be Parleela!

PARLEELA: Who is Parleela? A party girl who decides to fall in love on the first vacant Saturday night.

DICK CARNALL: Parleela is one who loves tonight and every night!

PARLEELA: The swinging sixties have gone. In this age of anxiety, we can do it no more.

DICK CARNALL: Let me disprove you!

PARLEELA: What is love?

DICK CARNALL: Don't ask. Just make it.

PARLEELA: Shall I feel love or analyse it?

DICK CARNALL: Feel me.

PARLEELA: Is love simple or complex?

DICK CARNALL: Come closer and I will tell you!

PARLEELA: You have a one-track mind.

DICK CARNALL: Don't involve the mind.

PARLEELA: That which is not driven by the mind is pure love. I must not listen to my mind. I must not think. Let myself go. Not control my

emotions. Fall for a penniless poet! Not for a
rich politician!

DICK CARNALL: Your endless meditation on love
makes me impatient.

PARLEELA: Can love be defined? Some say it can't be.

DICK CARNALL: Leave the philosophers. Come to me!

PARLEELA: Can love be fulfilled? Does it have to be
reciprocal? Can it be unconditional? Plato says
it is a search for wholeness! You read Plato.

DICK CARNALL: You read *Kama Sutra*!

PARLEELA: I read Derrida and I wonder whether I
love someone or something about someone?
Shall I differentiate between the who and the
what?

DICK CARNALL: De-romanticise love!

PARLEELA: What will love be like in the late 21st
century?

DICK CARNALL: A cocktail of hate and love.

PARLEELA: Where to find the heart-piercing love?

DICK CARNALL: The primacy of the heart ended with
the Enlightenment!

PARLEELA: Born of the Renaissance. Died of the
Enlightenment! The Brief History of Love!

DICK CARNALL: The Enlightenment was the antithesis of love.

PARLEELA: The Jesuits taught reason and undermined love.

DICK CARNALL: The Enlightenment liberated marriage from the Christian doctrine but reined in emotions.

PARLEELA: To be in love is to be on fire.

DICK CARNALL: Flesh flies in the face of Reason!

PARLEELA: Love is not a rational choice.

DICK CARNALL: Nor is sex. Scientists say the brain is shut off during an orgasm. If it is genuine, consciousness goes to sleep. No fear, no emotion can be felt during those moments. Free yourself from fear.

PARLEELA: Culture smothered the ecstasy of the body.

DICK CARNALL: It gave us ways to express ecstasy but diminished experience. Only the brainless can have pure pleasure.

PARLEELA: Culture robbed the English of physical pleasure.

DICK CARNALL: It drove pleasure underground. Turned it into perversion.

Parleela: Lady Chatterley sought to recover ecstasy from cultural niceties.

Dick Carnall: She revived passion. Inflamed women. Rocked marriages.

Parleela: Restored women's health.

Dick Carnall: *Lady Chatterley's Lover* heralded a cultural clash, a revolt against the Enlightenment.

Parleela: That's why this holy land outlawed *Lady Chatterley's Lover*.

Dick Carnall: *Tom Jones* caused a real earthquake!

Parleela: It doesn't cause a tremor anymore.

Dick Carnall: Because the earth here moves every second of night and day.

Parleela: In 21st century England, dalliance is the fruit of liberty.

Dick Carnall: Education is liberation.

Parleela: College girls do to their partners what schoolgirls are reluctant to do. Revealed a survey.

Dick Carnall: Because Henry Fielding is not taught in schools!

PARLEELA: There is a co-relation between education and sexual transgression! Education liberates. I will have more.

(Glasses tinkle)

DICK CARNALL: What has come over you? You are gulping down glass after glass! Enough for tonight! As you tell me.

PARLEELA: I'm sober. Dead sober!

DICK CARNALL: Then don't talk of heart!

PARLEELA: Don't talk at all?

DICK CARNALL. Move!

PARLEELA: I come from the East where a woman does not move.

DICK CARNALL: I make the first move. Move with me!

PARLEELA: Don't move. Stay.

DICK CARNALL: Say "I love you!" in Hindi.

PARLEELA: The two-and-a-half letters of love in Hindi remain unsaid.

DICK CARNALL: Then what do they say in Hindi?

PARLEELA: In Hindi, love means putting your heart into cooking for husband. Tell me what does it mean in English?

DICK CARNALL: Let me show you.

PARLEELA: Does love exist?

DICK CARNALL: Hidden in the jungle of hormones and pheromones.

PARLEELA: Can one transcend to a love beyond desire?

DICK CARNALL: There is no love beyond desire.

PARLEELA: Is love a myth? An illusion? A flight of fancy? A figment of the imagination? A rhetorical flourish? Just a pretext to bare the mind or the body!

DICK CARNALL: We need no pretext!

PARLEELA: Is love inspired by the narratives of exposure? A cultural construct based on one's biological and social conditioning. A chemical reaction? A feeling that comes and goes.

DICK CARNALL: You raise too many questions.

PARLEELA: Analyse love's anatomy. Its physics, chemistry, and engineering!

DICK CARNALL: Love is zero. As implied in the game of tennis. Let's do it.

PARLEELA: I think...

DICK CARNALL: Don't think. Thinking is lethal for love.

PARLEELA: I keep thinking...

DICK CARNALL: Keep thinking of love and you will grow old without it.

PARLEELA: Should I have faith in love?

DICK CARNALL: Just love love.

PARLEELA: Love overpowers faith.

DICK CARNALL: Love overpowers everything.

PARLEELA: Why do they say gut feeling when the heart does the feeling?

DICK CARNALL: You are an argumentative Indian!

PARLEELA: Is the heartbeat a function of love? How does the heart divide its work? What part pumps blood and what irrigates body and soul with feeling? Do blood and feeling race through the same veins? Does one flow continue when the other is choked? Can you be heart-dead?

DICK CARNALL: Being heart-dead is not the end of life. That is the beginning of a normal life.

PARLEELA: I dread the seductive tyranny of the ordinary. I dread the deadening pull of "appropriateness" and normalcy.

DICK CARNALL: I pull you towards the abnormal.

PARLEELA: I want to play-act. What shall I re-enact? Medieval love? Victorian love? Edwardian love? Contemporary love?

DICK CARNALL: Not digital love!

PARLEELA: Where shall I look for love? In a Shakespearean sonnet? In a Plath poem?

DICK CARNALL: Make love!

PARLEELA: Where, oh, where? On a park bench or in a bomb crater! Amidst ancient ruins or in a steel-glass tower! On a shiny marble lobby floor or in the dingy basement! In a submarine engine room! In an aircraft loo or in a car garage?

DICK CARNALL: Everywhere.

PARLEELA: What flavour? Possessive love? Othello-like love? Postmodern love? Bumper-sticker love? Advice-column love? Platonic love? The wandering minstrels' romantic love? Hanif Kureishi's seedy suburban love? The must-sleep with love? Angelic love? Can't-live-without-each-other love? Or just e-love?

DICK CARNALL: Have them all! Have them all!

PARLEELA: Gim-me-Gim-me-Gim-me!

DICK CARNALL: Take-Take-Take!

PARLEELA: You said all! Yes, I shall have all!

DICK CARNALL: Have them all!

PARLEELA: A woman-painter, a black rapper, a Jewish poet, an Irish novelist, a Dominican priest, a Hungarian violinist, a Nigerian nationalist, an Islamic scholar, a Tory bounder, a Labour leader, a Polish plumber, a Russian director, a French philosopher, a Spanish fighter, a German engineer, an American oilman, an Italian chef, and an Afghan Mujaheddin?

DICK CARNALL: A Romanian trapeze artist!

PARLEELA: Is there so much time to spare?

DICK CARNALL: For such a wide fare?

PARLEELA: And do I dare?

DICK CARNALL: Don't stand and stare! Begin with an affair.

PARLEELA: An affair begins with a person's nature, not actions.

DICK CARNALL: You like an affair.

PARLEELA: That way one doesn't form a tie. One who forms a tie is lost, Conrad cautions.

Dick Carnall: You won't be lost! I tie you up.

Parleela: Tie me up! Tie me down! Oh, to be the heroine of *Fifty Shades of Grey*!

Dick Carnall: Be Tess, Emma Bovary or Linda Lovelace but let's get on!

Parleela: Where is the romantic hero?

Dick Carnall: This is your problem. This is what reading does.

Parleela: I want to take all and at times, give up all. So, for two years a woman, for one year a sinner, for one month a nun, for one night a slut, for a few moments a penitent. I will be Moll.

Dick Carnall: Go through all the seven ages of woman. Have some more.

(Glasses tinkle)

Parleela: Give me! Give me! Divine love, demonic love, crazy love, dirty love, poetic love, plastic love, Platonic love! Give me all. The all of you! Am I a tramp? Am I a poet? Shall I go to the Hay Festival? Date a writer? Shall I go to the Venice Biennale? Sleep with a sculptor? On top of a hippopotamus in the exhibition hall!

Dick Carnall: You fantasise about art and literature, not men.

PARLEELA: I have a Wagnerian desire to escape. Escape myself!

DICK CARNALL: Escape with me! Fill my glass!

PARLEELA: Fill me up! If you keep gulping down, you will fall asleep!

DICK CARNALL: With you. Who wants to wake up when you sleep with me? *One, two, three four, five, six, seven / All good men go to heaven. One, two, three four, five, six, seven / All good men go to heaven. One, two, three four...*

CHAPTER THREE

Sauce of Life
MP's OFFICE

DICK CARNALL: Let me have another glass before we make it.

PARLEELA: Make what?

DICK CARNALL: Love.

PARLEELA: Love has no future. Artificial intelligence can pre-empt feeling. Robotics can make multiple copies of your love. In the internet age, old flames singe the new flames. Fragmented files burden the heart. Without a crap cleaner, the heart gets damaged.

DICK CARNALL: *The Death of the Heart.*

PARLEELA: Is there more to life than love?

DICK CARNALL: Without love, there is no life.

PARLEELA: Is love spontaneous or a matter of habit? Is love a child of circumstances? Conditioned by the alternatives available at a given time?

DICK CARNALL: Loving is not questioning.

PARLEELA: Only the First Love is genuine. Then on, it is a well-rehearsed drill, contrived to the core. Scheming and artifice.

DICK CARNALL: I could do with a second helping of the first love!

PARLEELA: Will England destroy my faith in love? Will I return to India, the way Forster's Mrs Moore had to return from India?

DICK CARNALL: She was travestied into EsmissEsmoor.

PARLEELA: I don't want to return to India to die.

DICK CARNALL: Not while I am alive. Time to reveal yourself in full glory.

PARLEELA: Don't be obscene. "You'll shock the folks of Golders Green."

DICK CARNALL: They produce bosomy girls with curls and pearls.

PARLEELA: I read you like an open book.

DICK CARNALL: You the inscrutable Orient. Lay yourself open to me!

PARLEELA: Do I dare? Do I dare to eat peach or lie on a beach?

DICK CARNALL: Come fly with me!

PARLEELA: My wings are scorched. Time stands still.

DICK CARNALL: *Tempus fugit,* when you are with me.

PARLEELA: I want to escape to another world.

DICK CARNALL: To do what you can't do in this one. Sheer cowardice!

PARLEELA: We are all cowards. Even the writers want home security with the flights of fancy. Indian wives write to sublimate their desire. I burn with imagination. What comes next?

DICK CARNALL: Action! This is no conversation assembly. Let's taste the forbidden fruit! Fill my glass! I am ready to fill you!

(Glasses tinkle)

PARLEELA: Do you find me exotic?

DICK CARNALL: I do.

PARLEELA: I find you exotic!

DICK CARNALL: Two lovers of exotica!

PARLEELA: Bill Clinton found a Jewish girl exotic. He famously asked her what kind of name Lewinski is.

DICK CARNALL: Your blue Krishna woos white milkmaids. They are exotic to him; he is exotic to them.

PARLEELA: I'm a black Gopi and you a white Krishna!

DICK CARNALL: The opposites attract.

PARLEELA: You people like dusky beauties. Indian men like white women.

DICK CARNALL: Indian women like gods.

PARLEELA: I want to be Mira, the Rajput princess who surrenders.

DICK CARNALL: I am ready to accept. Let's have more.

(Glasses tinkle)

PARLEELA: Wooing is preparing the face to meet another face.

DICK CARNALL: Art is artifice.

PARLEELA: You are contriving. I am contriving. I'm *fictio.* I don't like it. Things should just happen. I shouldn't have to plan, make choices and decisions. Seduction requires planning. Selection negates spontaneity, authenticity.

DICK CARNALL: What is authenticity? It is judged by subjectivity.

PARLEELA: I would like to be written about as *The Woman of Feeling*. But my feeling does not last.

DICK CARNALL: Let me feel you!

PARLEELA: Peel me! I shall indulge myself. Why shouldn't I?

DICK CARNALL: Now you're talking!

PARLEELA: I can reason with reason but can't fight emotion.

DICK CARNALL: Cognitive research has undermined emotion. Linked it to intelligence.

PARLEELA: I'm not embarrassed by emotion.

DICK CARNALL: Come naked clean!

PARLEELA: Peel away my ambiguity. Flake away my dilemma. Remove my reason. Reveal the real me. Sweep me off my feet. Take me to the moon. Come, my demon lover! Come!

DICK CARNALL: Here I come!

PARLEELA: Wait! First tell me if love is independent of the object of love. His virtues, vices, and the colour of his skin, the look on his face, the way he smiles, and the way he walks?

DICK CARNALL: Ask no questions and don't hold yourself back.

PARLEELA: Is love a mood? Love on the rebound? Love on the run? Courtly love? How to test love? Is love at first sight, the real love?

DICK CARNALL: Never fall for the first site. Keep clicking!

PARLEELA: Shall I be 'sick of love', singing the Song of Solomon? Or shall I follow the new edition and 'faint with love'?

DICK CARNALL: Don't involve a sacred text, for God's sake!

PARLEELA: Human attraction comes in different forms. I can be held or distracted, fixed, or unsettled. How does one fall in love? Inside out or outside in?

DICK CARNALL: "Woman, if you gotta ask, you'll never know."

PARLEELA: A good quote!

DICK CARNALL: A well-read woman will theorise, not fall.

PARLEELA: To hell with my conditioning. I want to fall.

DICK CARNALL: Is this conversation fake?

PARLEELA: Trust me, as you would say.

Dick Carnall: Are you just researching love? Working on a book that critics will call "a meditation on love"!

Parleela: I'm thinking of the unthinking love!

Dick Carnall: Your *mind* is not what I'm after!

Parleela: My mind lost its virginity. The slate is not blank. I can only overwrite.

Dick Carnall: Cover your mind, bare your body. Give me all!

Parleela: Stop tickling me. I must tell you all.

Dick Carnall: I'm all ears. And more.

Parleela: My childhood was double-shaded. A traditional mother, an Anglicised father. The father liked the western toilet and the mother prayed in the home temple. We ate with fork and knife but talked in the mother tongue. I was sent to a convent school with an Indian meal in my tiffin box. My classmates brought sandwiches and found my lunch funny. I decided to be one up to take revenge. I got a boyfriend and learnt to play the piano!

Dick Carnall: That was a life-changing experience.

Parleela: I became an exile in my country. I memorised the *Acts of the Apostles*, sang *Home on the Range*, and crossed my heart. My father, like the English, considered it a bad form to show emotions. India's high cultural tradition. I was not kissed by my father or mother! Nor did I see them kissing.

DICK CARNALL: Then how did you start fantasising? There was no reference point. From whom did you get the idea?

PARLEELA: From books.

DICK CARNALL: Did sex come before romance? Were you married off to an old cousin when you were 12?

PARLEELA: You read *Bradford News*! I don't come from a Pakistani family! You homogenise the Asians.

DICK CARNALL: I'm sorry.

PARLEELA: I got kissed in my school years. The first kiss-giver fumbled. The second went through. I graduated and entered a *marriage de raison*. In six weeks, I realised that the Christian concept of marriage was not for me. I rescued myself from that arranged mess. Liaisons followed, forged in the heat of the moment. They all turned tragic, one after another.

DICK CARNALL: Tonight we write a new chapter in your life.

PARLEELA: I started dreaming of fens and glens and seagulls. Floating in the mist, dancing among the daffodils. A long story!

DICK CARNALL: Tell me! Tell me!

PARLEELA: I saw my older sister trapped in middle-class mediocrity and stale stability of a small town! Saw her struggling with the events of daily life—teaching English literature, cutting vegetables, washing lentils, cooking rice, buying fruits, making beds, humouring the husband, disciplining daughters, readying the mother-in-law's idols and the father-in-law's hot water bottle.

DICK CARNALL: Who was responsible for her misery?

PARLEELA: It was her own fault. She said yes to an arranged marriage. Refused a Princeton fellowship. She could have lived in a mixed dorm. Smoked and tried Ecstasy. Done her PhD. Married a Jewish painter or a Polish plumber. Written a novel, won fame. Been a photographer or a pornographer of great distinction. But she chose India. She thinks family is more precious than individual net worth. She is drunk on the spirit of sacrifice.

DICK CARNALL: I bet your sister is happy.

PARLEELA: Strangely, she *is* happy.

DICK CARNALL: You abandoned India!

PARLEELA: I was not going to fast and pray. Pour water on a stone Shiva and chant: "May I be a wife like Sita." "May I have a husband like Rama?" I had already read D H Lawrence!

DICK CARNALL: *Lady Chatterley's Lover* was not banned in India!

PARLEELA: I could neither be a wife without a room of one's own, nor a wife with a room of one's own. Not a starving wife. Not a diamond-necklaced wife. I saw both kinds. Those scrapping the bottom of the rice vessel and those married to filthy rich man. In the latter's world, a wife envied a mistress.

DICK CARNALL: Your sister has her husband's love.

PARLEELA: A husband's love is not the be-all and end-all. Let her be happy with his love. I can't imagine myself doing what she does. Living with daily drudgery, a life without adventure, excitement, fun.

DICK CARNALL: You came to England to have fun? We went to India to have fun!

PARLEELA: London mounts plays, passions, orgies.

DICK CARNALL: Is that how London is seen in India?

PARLEELA: Life here is liberating, never boring. Have flings. Marry. Divorce. Remarry. Fresh lovers, ex's, and ex-ex's and triple Xs. An old flame refires the embers of your heart. You split, remarry and then re-divorce. Break up to be whole again!

DICK CARNALL: Let's be one whole!

(Glasses tinkle)

PARLEELA: I'm possessed by carnal cynicism, titillated by theory, amused by play-acting. Here I'm out every night! In India, as cows come home and the evening falls, it is sleepy silence and deadly darkness.

DICK CARNALL: In darkness, I turn you on!

PARLEELA: I dreamt of flying away with a knight on a white horse. Being rescued by a gallant love-maker. Oh to be an English heroine! You fall in love; marry a "bounder" and then a rich husband, to be ensconced in a country mansion. My aunt studied in Cambridge and married an Englishman to escape the Indian dullness. She became the Marchioness of Winchester. She was my role model.

DICK CARNALL: Every woman cannot be a Lady!

PARLEELA: Madonna reinvented herself as Lady of the Manor!

DICK CARNALL: An upstart Romanian bought a manor house!

PARLEELA: Life in England appeared richer and fuller. I wanted English adventures. A schoolgirl here shares drinks and intimacy with Richard Burton. Before reaching 16, she experiences lovers, pregnancies, indifferent husbands, drunkard mother, cruel father, lecherous stepfather, helpful healer. She sails through unions and partings, disasters, and recovery, achieving a brilliant professional success. Leads a full life. What a contrast to the dull life in India!

DICK CARNALL: You didn't believe in virginity?

PARLEELA: I believed in drama, adventure, suspense, suffering and illegitimacy.

DICK CARNALL: We will get on famously. Planting love children is my hobby!

PARLEELA: I joined the battle between tradition and modernity, between desire and reticence. I ended the last "imprudent" marriage, turned my back on my old world and set out on my individual journey.

DICK CARNALL: Did you get what you wanted?

PARLEELA: Flying higher and higher, I burnt my wings and fell on the earth.

Dick Carnall: Icarus Girl!

Parleela: I wasn't defeated. I crawled out of my hell and went to Oxford, to feel. To be a poet. Too much of life pre-empted literature. Didn't get to commit my feelings to paper!

Dick Carnall: Writing would not have paid.

Parleela: That is consoling. Why rearrange words, change letters, delete commas, insert full stops, correct sentences, refine phrases, restructure paragraphs, retune thoughts, stress ideas, suppress sense, edit emotions? Juggle with characters all the time.

Dick Carnall: So where or what are you now?

Parleela: Literature goes, life goes on. I don't look at the rainbow. I don't dream of daffodils. I think of my mother's home temple and its little gods.

Dick Carnall: That's called growing up. The young have immunity to spirituality that the old catch easily.

Parleela: I am stricken with second thoughts. I always re-examine my position.

Dick Carnall: Try the reverse missionary position.

Parleela: Nothing makes sense.

DICK CARNALL: The centre cannot hold. Fill my glass!

(Glasses tinkle)

PARLEELA: Here. Cheers!

DICK CARNALL: Cheers!

PARLEELA: How do I know myself? I can't be my sister. What shall I be?

DICK CARNALL: All one's life, one tries to be someone else or not be someone else.

PARLEELA: Depressing talk, this.

DICK CARNALL: Let's have a breath of fresh air. I take you in a church.

PARLEELA: Churches are for praying.

DICK CARNALL: A graveyard is a private place.

PARLEELA: There I hate to embrace!

DICK CARNALL: In your culture, the sacred and sensual are interconnected.

PARLEELA: Yes, the religious, aesthetic, and practical lives are one.

DICK CARNALL: You enjoyed all that was forbidden to us.

PARLEELA: Just because our temples have erotic statues. Your Bible too has sacred erotica! Read the Song of Songs.

DICK CARNALL: Are you superstitious or westernised?

PARLEELA: You want to have it both ways. Why don't you decide whether respecting the sanctity of church is westernisation or superstition?

DICK CARNALL: Priests are worse than MPs, in matters of sex.

PARLEELA: They're human! Priests do it. Sexuality, like politics, is existential.

DICK CARNALL: The combination is explosive.

PARLEELA: That is what the tabloids believe.

DICK CARNALL: We MPs do it due to political pressures, late-night sessions, comely researchers, and separation from families.

PARLEELA: Any excuse for cheating wives.

DICK CARNALL: Let's cheat!

PARLEELA: I have no one to cheat. I can't have freedom *from*.

DICK CARNALL: You can have freedom *to*. Two of us make a couple. A simple sum. *One, two, three four, five, six seven / All good men go to heaven.*

PARLEELA: Women?

DICK CARNALL: Good girls go to heaven; bad girls go everywhere.

PARLEELA: Let's go everywhere.

DICK CARNALL: Everywhere is here. You are here with me. The embraceable me. Let copulation thrive. I'm thirsty. Give me more.

(A glass bangs on the table. Sound of glasses being filled)

PARLEELA: Here you go! Ouch! What are you doing? You're hurting me.

DICK CARNALL: A cinematic cliché! Like a film heroine, you say this without meaning it!

PARLEELA: You are pulling me too hard! You are breathing too hot!

DICK CARNALL: I blow hot, I blow cold. I am not old, I'm bold!

PARLEELA: You cannot hold!

DICK CARNALL: Let's waltz! Our waltzing in India mystified the natives. One fellow asked: Why do they move fast and then walk slowly? "Because

the missus has to be made hot first, then
cooled," he was told. We're the dancing Tories!

PARLEELA: This is no Conservative Ball.

DICK CARNALL: I get your red knickers in a twist.

PARLEELA: I have no knickers, red or blue.

DICK CARNALL: So much the better, my dear.

PARLEELA: You are drunk. Beware of Lord Nolan!

DICK CARNALL: He has no teeth. You have beautiful
teeth. I touch these by my tongue.

PARLEELA: You have had your tongue down my
throat.

DICK CARNALL: I want it literally.

PARLEELA: Beware of the Prime Minister's Back-to-
Basics campaign.

DICK CARNALL: Let us get down to the basics.

PARLEELA: Is the Minister for the Prevention of Sex
Scandals your friend?

DICK CARNALL: I will be transparent. I will enter you
in the MPs' register as my personal interest.

PARLEELA: Personal becomes public. We will land
up on the Front Page. That will be the end of
your prime ministerial dream!

DICK CARNALL: Beware of Rex! He sells oppressed women's stories. Keep away from the rouge editors. One editor wormed his way into the heart of a dusky parliamentary researcher and then let her down. She retaliated with the fury of a woman scorned. She cut off the arms of his coat and legs of his trousers.

PARLEELA: She was a kind Indian. A Liverpool woman tore off a delicate body part of her ex-lover and tried to swallow it!

DICK CARNALL: The Indian woman scratched the famous editor.

PARLEELA: Scratch a foe, find a lover!

DICK CARNALL: The editor's career did not get a scratch. He went from newspaper to newspaper!

PARLEELA: That Indian woman recovered without a shrink. She caught an agent and milked her celebrity status.

DICK CARNALL: She was the original 'Asian Babe'.

The first Crossover Hit. India's lead was followed by Bangladesh. Faria's name will be written in golden letters in the history of the Football Association.

PARLEELA: I resent your stereotyping the Asian women.

DICK CARNALL: Faria tried to be English! An Asian beauty doesn't bed and tell! Will you ever sell my love to the *Sun*?

PARLEELA: If someone were to barge in now, what will he see?

DICK CARNALL: What will he see? You're dressed. I'm dressed.

PARLEELA: But I'm Asian, you're English. And who will believe we are talking of literature?

DICK CARNALL: The drama of false appearances. Their aberrant viewing will enhance our forbidden desires.

PARLEELA: You are idiotically profound. Profoundly idiotic!

DICK CARNALL: The effect of observer on the observed. Their misperception will release our repressed desire. Their gaze will make us perform exactly as they imagined. If they see us undressed and tangled, we will be so.

PARLEELA: We are different from each other! Race matters. They will not see you pawing me. They will see me manipulating you. If I cry, they won't trust my tears. Women columnists will go after me like hyenas. They will exonerate you but call me names!

DICK CARNALL: I enjoy their confidence!

PARLEELA: Were I English, they would see me as a victim. A victim of male exploitation.

DICK CARNALL: An Asian Babe is safer! Pamela can bring me down. Parleela won't!

CHAPTER FOUR

Oriental Fantasy
MP's OFFICE

DICK CARNALL: Look what I got for you from Paris.

PARLEELA: Oh, how beautiful! Thank you! You went to Paris without me? Did you take your wife?

DICK CARNALL: Sheikh Mohammad wanted me to come alone. This time it was all business.

PARLEELA: Is what we are doing not business?

DICK CARNALL: A parliamentary affair, mandated by Westminster's tradition.

PARLEELA: Fill my cup!

DICK CARNALL: I will. Come! I'm on your mind.

PARLEELA: You know my mind!

DICK CARNALL: Knowing you is in my genes.

PARLEELA: White man knows the non-whites better then they themselves.

DICK CARNALL: Knowing is done. Come to doing!

PARLEELA: In planes we do it.

DICK CARNALL: In trains we do it.

PARLEELA: On graves we do it.

DICK CARNALL: Underground we do it.

PARLEELA: In the open air we do it.

DICK CARNALL: Behind closed doors we do it.

PARLEELA: Princes do it.

DICK CARNALL: Paupers do it.

PARLEELA: Birds of Kew do it.

DICK CARNALL: Bees of Buckingham do it.

PARLEELA: Baboons of Balham do it!

DICK CARNALL: Moths of Manchester do it!

PARLEELA: MPs of London do it.

DICK CARNALL: Congressmen of Washington do it.

PARLEELA: Presidents in the White House do it.

DICK CARNALL: We in Parliament House do it!

PARLEELA: We don't!

DICK CARNALL: (*banging glass*) Some more, please! Let's play the game of love!

PARLEELA: You are in no condition to do anything. Alcohol has cooled your passion.

DICK CARNALL: Try me.

PARLEELA: I see your political future sinking in the glass. You may have to resign as the Parliamentary Affairs Minister.

DICK CARNALL: I *am* ministering a parliamentary affair!

PARLEELA: I am not one of your members. You don't know me.

DICK CARNALL: We have known you for long. We wrote on India's charming damsels.

PARLEELA: And left your imprint on them.

DICK CARNALL: In the 18th century, we found you to be better than the English ladies who were "immoderately fond of dancing".

PARLEELA: Indian women came to you as a refreshing change.

DICK CARNALL: Once the British soldier tasted the Burma girl, he found 'ousemaids of London wanting!

PARLEELA: English housemaids faced tough competition!

DICK CARNALL: I quote: "Ask your own heart if an Indian damsel just risen from the limpid bath in all the native charms of cleanliness and artless beauty, is not much more likely to inspire you with sentiments of desire and love."

PARLEELA: So you liked Indian women for their bathing habits! The unclean English ladies put you off!

DICK CARNALL: An English poet said: "This Englishwoman is so refined / She has no bosom and not behind."

PARLEELA: English women felt threatened in India.

DICK CARNALL: Not by the dark men but by dusky

Indian women. Their men were ensnared by Oriental beauties. The English wives had competition.

PARLEELA: The English wives had reasons to be nervous. Look at the British Begums, immortalised in portraits. And look at your wives.

DICK CARNALL: In Waugh's *Black Mischief,* the African says, "It must be very sad for the English gentlemen to marry English ladies."

PARLEELA: Home-grown pallor ill-compared with foreign-burnished copper. Consequently, the

British wives were neglected and native women abused.

DICK CARNALL: Lady Clementi preferred tea to sex! Riots in marriage-beds were common.

PARLEELA: So, you people liked Indian women!

DICK CARNALL: Men too.

PARLEELA: Jeremy Seabrooke lamented that the British and Indian gays did not start a cross-cultural dialogue until 2005.

DICK CARNALL: The British Empire was driven by sex and technology, greed and power, discontent, and dream. My forefathers served in India. Liaison with Hindoo women is in my blood. I can't help it!

PARLEELA: That's what Diana's lover said, blaming his father and grandfather for what he did.

DICK CARNALL: I can't help it!

PARLEELA: Your liaisons were superficial. You never went for an Indian bride. Neither a nautch girl of Cawnpore nor a Princess of Jaipur. Your Royals, for matrimonial purposes, preferred silly little countries of Europe rather than an old civilisation like India! The Moguls were better.

DICK CARNALL: In the early years of the encounter, we did go for the Indian *Bibis.* Some liaisons were formalised. They bore fruit: Poor *Gulab* now was in *that* way, /That those who 'love their Lords' should be; /And in a week, to *Qui Hi*'s joy/ Produced our youth a chopping boy.

PARLEELA: In that phase, it was a productive Indo-British encounter!

DICK CARNALL: That was in 1780. Many Englishmen married Muslim girls. They converted to Islam, got circumcised and produced lovely children. The Begums were remembered in the wills. Then the British management cracked down. The East India Company excluded from employment the children of British men with Indian wives.

PARLEELA: How heartless!

DICK CARNALL: Initially, our encounter was human. Later, the interracial love could not speak its name.

PARLEELA: The Englishman who tried to marry a young widow of Lahore was wounded at the most delicate spot so that he could never marry. The girl's hands were cut off.

DICK CARNALL: That was a typical case of "Beyond the Pale". Sexual taboos maintained the racial division of a colonial society. We enforced these as soon as we became a confident superpower.

PARLEELA: As the East appeared vanquished, the relationship changed.

DICK CARNALL: Liaisons with the natives were now considered shameful and scandalous.

PARLEELA: Did any English princess marry an Indian?

DICK CARNALL: The terms of trade changed in the 18th century. No Indian would have liked to marry an English woman then. Similarly, we didn't consider it proper. The British renegades had to take Muslim names. Sergeant James Snelling became Sultaun!

PARLEELA: The Bangalore captives!

DICK CARNALL: Some Britishers transgressed and transformed themselves! Colonel "Hindoo" Stewart of Bengal wrote a book. William Fraser, who went to India in the 1800s, acquired seven Indian wives. He had numerous children, Hindu as well as Muslim, depending on their mamas.

PARLEELA: Weird encounters! Multi-culturalism was at play long before it got its name!

DICK CARNALL: Editor John Maxwell had an Indian wife. James Skinner, the Scot who built a church in Delhi, took a Rajput Princess.

PARLEELA: The tale of Achilles Kirkpatrick and Khair un-Nisaa of Hyderabad has been told by William Dalrymple in *The White Mughals.*

DICK CARNALL: Sir David Ochterlony used to show off every evening on Delhi's streets his 13 Indian wives!

PARLEELA: Dalrymple digs up such cases to praise British "tolerance" of "the other". Dalrymple loves inter-cultural liaisons.

DICK CARNALL: Pity, the White Moguls have gone! Oh, to be a White Mogul! One man, 13 wives!

PARLEELA: Did such couples live happily ever after?

DICK CARNALL: Unfortunately, no.

PARLEELA: They merely mingled and multiplied.

DICK CARNALL: The love stories of my forefathers are coming out!

PARLEELA: What about the English women? You said they found Indian men attractive but there aren't many stories about their liaisons.

DICK CARNALL: Our women in India were heavily guarded. The white male feared native molestation.

PARLEELA: Victorian values turned sexual acts into "transgression".

DICK CARNALL: Mere suspicion of female impropriety could be tragic. For the English women, everything was considered improper! In 1882, Mary Pigot got involved with a fellow teacher, a Christian named Baboo Kalicharan Banerjee. They went to a church picnic in Calcutta's Barrackpore Park where they allegedly touched each other. It was a big scandal. Miss Pigot fought the slander and was exonerated by the court.

PARLEELA: Did any Maharaja manage to seduce a lady or a chambermaid in Buckingham Palace?

DICK CARNALL: The rapacious Maharajas kept their own women in purdah and played with hired European concubines in hotels on the Strand. An Indian Maharaja was caught in bed in Paris with one Mrs Robinson.

PARLEELA: These were women of ill repute.

DICK CARNALL: Any English woman marrying a Maharaja was called "wicked". Our women found Indian men raffish and lascivious. The

Memsahibs, who saw romance under a pugree, were tempted but felt controlled by tradition.

PARLEELA: Your women's sexuality scared you.

DICK CARNALL: We suppressed it by frightening them about the savage natives.

PARLEELA: Had the English women been allowed to mix with Indians, they would have created a bond between the two peoples.

DICK CARNALL: For quite long, we were able to protect white virtue.

PARLEELA: Till the arrival of the pill and the swinging sixties. Till your women got liberated by *Sex and the City* and the suburbia began to seethe with desperate housewives.

DICK CARNALL: Multi-culturalism sullied white virtue.

PARLEELA: In early British India, there was cross-cultural dialogue. An English missionary admired the Hindu scriptures and thought of replacing the Old Testament with them to "raise up the Hindoo!"

DICK CARNALL: When they first went to India, the English officers used to prostrate themselves in Mogul courts. They admired the Indian war fighting capability, scholarship, and the legal system.

PARLEELA: The Britishers in India merrily ate *chapati* till the mutiny of 1857 but after that they shunned it. From then on it was only leavened bread! The exploitative phase began.

DICK CARNALL: Mutual appreciation was gone.

PARLEELA: The wise wealthy Orient began to be seen as poor, weak, vile, and ignorant. The earlier history was blacked out.

DICK CARNALL: Once they gained complete control of India, the British became arrogant.

PARLEELA: The West's interaction with China followed the same course. Began with the Era of Deference. Then came the Era of Contempt. And then the Era of Paternalism.

DICK CARNALL: The relationship with Indians changed as London got frightened of the officers' proclivity to assimilate and catch localitis. It suppressed the tendency with a heavy hand. Banned the British Begums.

PARLEELA: That was tragic.

DICK CARNALL: It didn't last. Ultimately, we went beyond the pale and pierced the veil in the name of multiculturalism.

PARLEELA: Now *Asian Babe* is everywhere!

DICK CARNALL: And you are with me.

PARLEELA: And you are with me!

DICK CARNALL: An English diplomat married a Delhi girl, daughter of a big businessman.

PARLEELA: He couldn't have married a sweeper's daughter. Your wretched class system!

DICK CARNALL: Lady Chatterley defied it.

PARLEELA: Your Queen had a soft corner for a humble Indian.

DICK CARNALL: The Queen had no soft corner! The frigid old girl with whacky children.

PARLEELA: I am talking of the Queen who had an Indian *munim.*

DICK CARNALL: The last Prince had an Indian *hakim*!

PARLEELA: Queen Victoria's most favoured servant was Munshi Karim.

DICK CARNALL: A film turned Queen Victoria into *Mrs Brown.*

PARLEELA: *Mrs Karim* would have flopped then but she appeared in that avatar years later after an Indian woman wrote a book on the two.

DICK CARNALL: Karim was a Muslim.

PARLEELA: Your women have a thing about Muslims.

DICK CARNALL: Quite unfortunate! Post 7/7, an English girl will find it hard to take a Muslim lover.

PARLEELA: Jemima, Diana, and the earlier generation that went to British India, all preferred Muslims. Jemima married a Pathan cricketer. Diana had a crush on a Pakistani heart surgeon.

DICK CARNALL: She had more than a crush on an Egyptian Muslim!

PARLEELA: That crush led to a crash.

DICK CARNALL: Princess Diana's charmed circle included a British army officer, an actor, a rugby captain, a Canadian rocker, a Pakistani heart surgeon, an Indian businessman and the Egyptian playboy!

PARLEELA: But her final dream was built around a Muslim. Atavistic national memory! Miss Adela Quested was awakened to her savage sexuality, not by Pandit Ajit but by Dr Aziz.

DICK CARNALL: Muslims are considered more virile.

PARLEELA: It could be a religious thing. Your God is closer to Allah than to Brahma!

DICK CARNALL: You may be right. Samuel Johnson said: "There are two objects of curiosity, the Christian and the Mahometan." All the rest may be considered barbarous."

PARLEELA: The patriotic English women perhaps followed the British government's strategy of divide and rule. They took Muslim lovers to make Hindus jealous!

DICK CARNALL: Several Englishmen went for Hindu women. Anthony Firangi of Calcutta was a devotee of the Goddess Kali.

PARLEELA: Hindu women were reserved and hard to penetrate.

DICK CARNALL: Behind the veil, Muslim girls were freer and less virtuous.

PARLEELA: Muslim girls had orthodoxy to rebel against.

DICK CARNALL: As you rebelled against the convent upbringing to walk into my arms!

PARLEELA: You mean, had I been a Sharmila, I wouldn't be touching you!

DICK CARNALL: I saw you and realised what the Englishmen in India saw in the native women!

PARLEELA: The English wives in India were "painted corpses". High-class English girls were trained to shun an unrehearsed emotion.

DICK CARNALL: The English woman did her duty in bed without putting her heart into it.

PARLEELA: No wonder American women attracted English men.

DICK CARNALL: The young hero of *Love, Actually* dumps Britain for America to get girls.

PARLEELA: Prince William was enchanted by American *Girls Gone Wild.*

DICK CARNALL: Another Prince went further. He could not find a bride in Britain!

PARLEELA: Mrs Wallis Simpson, the Baltimore divorcee, got your King to call her "Mummie".

PARLEELA: Mrs Catherine Walston caught Graham Greene.

DICK CARNALL: Churchill's father married Jennnie Jerome of the Bronx.

PARLEELA: Sir Harold Macmillan too had an American mother!

DICK CARNALL: American women chased us for our titles.

PARLEELA: You chased them for their dollars.

DICK CARNALL: Britain needed dollars after the War!

PARLEELA: The eighth Duke of Marlborough electrified his Blenheim from the proceeds of his American marriage.

DICK CARNALL: The ninth Duke married fabulously rich Consuelo Vanderbilt.

PARLEELA: You used them. They used you!

DICK CARNALL: The transatlantic special relationship was built on personal sacrifices. It paid back when the war came.

PARLEELA: The Americans did to you what you do to other countries. Plant brides to influence foreign policy. Just as you drafted English girls for the Middle Eastern potentates. Promoted romances for political, strategic, and commercial interests. The Americans sent Hope Cook to the Chogyal of Sikkim, allegedly to make him want to break away from India.

DICK CARNALL: You will claim that the Rajiv-Sonia romance in Cambridge was inspired by MI 5!

PARLEELA: The English language continues to influence India's destiny long after the English were gone. It was for learning English that

Italian Sonia came to Cambridge where she met Rajiv Gandhi!

DICK CARNALL: Our Royals had intimate ties with Indian ruling families but it never led to a high-profile liaison.

PARLEELA: No Maharaja's wife was ever courted and wed by an Englishman!

DICK CARNALL: In the twenties, there were rumours about the raffish Prince of Wales and an Indian Maharani. The King's displeasure was conveyed to the lady through the India Office. She was asked to leave England.

PARLEELA: Is an account available in the official archives?

DICK CARNALL: Several tons of files containing private information about the princely families were burnt before India was granted independence. We did not want the princes to be blackmailed by Indian politicians.

PARLEELA: You paid back your benefactors. Britain was in debt of Indian Princes. The Raja of Benares donated money for digging a well in Oxfordshire for your drought-stricken poor. The Kohinoor came as a "gift". Many English institutions survived on donations from India. For all this and 300 years of shared history, not one prestigious liaison to show!

DICK CARNALL: I'm ready to make up.

PARLEELA: When the Queen rode a chariot with the Maharaja of Jaipur, the Pink City crowds fantasised about the handsome pair. The Queen could have forged an alliance fit for a thrilling English opera.

DICK CARNALL: It wouldn't have worked. Diana returned empty from Pakistan. Jemima could not carry on.

PARLEELA: The dusky sons of Hindostan have become acceptable, at least for trial runs! Liz Hurley picked up an Indian and was with him for some time.

DICK CARNALL: That's modern Britain. Lady Davina Windsor married a Maori. White girls now take black lovers!

PARLEELA: "Brixton Brides" galore!

DICK CARNALL: We started buying in Brixton and mingling with them in bedrooms. Thus began the decline of the Master Race.

PARLEELA: Scientists now say that race is biologically meaningless.

DICK CARNALL: Race has given you the colour of your skin and the texture of your nipples!

PARLEELA: Go on. Fetishise my lips! Orientalise me! You and I can never meet.

DICK CARNALL: You need your idols to carry on a spiritual dialogue.

PARLEELA: You need the Other to carry on a dialectical struggle.

DICK CARNALL: And yet the Brown Sahibs and White Mughals are part of our shared history.

PARLEELA: Don't trust historians. The Indian rope trick was a hoax! The story was cooked up to ridicule the Orient. The *Chicago Daily Tribune* printed it in 1890. Later they admitted it had all been made up. History was falsified.

DICK CARNALL: We are revising it.

PARLEELA: Distorting it further!

DICK CARNALL: A new debate on the British Empire is raging. The new history will focus on the Empire's beauty.

PARLEELA: We swallowed the lies written to justify colonial rule. Tagore was so critical of the Indian history written by British scholars.

DICK CARNALL: We saved you from a false historical and cultural consciousness.

PARLEELA: It is said that India has no known history! The course of India's history was always determined by external forces. You annexed our past because in it you saw your own very distant past!

DICK CARNALL: History happens only in the West.

PARLEELA: On the contrary, Rushdie says you English don't know your history because much of it happened overseas!

DICK CARNALL: Colonial history is fiction. I agree.

PARLEELA: Most English academics do a hatchet job to damn my people.

DICK CARNALL: Hollywood plays with British history to show us in bad light.

PARLEELA: Indian historians will undo the mischief!

DICK CARNALL: Are there any Indian historians?

PARLEELA: An infinite variety. Nationalist historians, Marxist historians, Hindutva historians, Dalit historians, school textbook historians. There are revisionist, interpretativist and empiricist historians.

DICK CARNALL: Samuel Johnson said all the colouring, all the philosophy of history is confection!

PARLEELA: What does it matter when facts are *passé*!

DICK CARNALL: Some say we created the Orient to define the Enlightenment!

PARLEELA: In the eyes of the West, the 'Other' is not just feminine; it is backward, weak, inferior, absurd, passive, and ready to be dominated.

DICK CARNALL: Above all, the "Other" is sensual.

PARLEELA: Do I exude Orientalness?

DICK CARNALL: I love your ideological mutterings! You sound like the heroine of *Bride and Prejudice*!

PARLEELA: The libidinisation of the Orient degrades me. Your eyes break up my body.

DICK CARNALL: I observe you with longing, not curiosity.

PARLEELA: Your epistemic assaults failed due to India's unknowability. You measured our skulls but couldn't map our souls!

DICK CARNALL: I will map your body!

PARLEELA: Don't exoticise me.

DICK CARNALL: Your own Indians do it.

PARLEELA: Our writers must do it to get the English readers! It is worse when others do it.

DICK CARNALL: You should feel flattered that you appear exotic!

PARLEELA: It's not about me. You want to penetrate the Great Indian Mystery, reach the heart of a dark mysterious land! I will not be dragged to the colonial couch!

DICK CARNALL: I take you on the post-colonial couch!

PARLEELA: Can we not have a mainstream-type engagement? Like between you and Laura, you and Anne and you and Sarah?

DICK CARNALL: I feel at ease with you.

PARLEELA: The ageing man feels more secure with an Oriental woman!

DICK CARNALL: The Sarahs are not spicy. *Nutmeg and ginger, cinnamon and clove / That's what gave me my jolly red nose.* It is for spices that we went to India. Paradise smells of spices!

PARLEELA: The Church considered spices lustful and pagan even though Christ's body was anointed with spices.

DICK CARNALL: You are my pagan goddess!

PARLEELA: Your aromatic Spice Girl!

DICK CARNALL: Come!

PARLEELA: Exoticism has been crucial to the East-West relations. An instrument of emblematic power over the other. That's why you chase exotica!

DICK CARNALL: Rhymes with erotica!

PARLEELA: Don't will the Eroticism Doctrine over me just because I'm weak.

DICK CARNALL: Your front is firm!

PARLEELA: The East-West encounter is comic! You go there looking for bare breasts. The Indians come here to ogle at them!

DICK CARNALL: You make me a victim of Occidentalism!

PARLEELA: Malcolm Muggeridge, during his Kerala stay, watched women bathing in village ponds. He must have gone beyond staring, considering how he chased his friends' wives in England.

DICK CARNALL: Muggeridge said the great quest of his life was not virtue but sin.

PARLEELA: The nunnery and brothel are traditionally yoked together in the English imagination.

Dick Carnall: Muggeridge saw life as an eternal battle between two irreconcilable opposites, "the world of the flesh and the world of the spirit". He played with both spheres.

Parleela: Muggeridge wrote on the bare breasts of Kerala women.

Dick Carnall: I am ready to write on yours. Let me take out my pencil. Better than Salman Rushdie's.

Parleela: You don't *write* with your pencil.

Dick Carnall: I am writing *Raj in the Bed,* a sequel to *Raj at the Table*. It examines the linkage between the carnal pursuit and imperial power.

Parleela: A book on colonial homoeroticism has just come out. You stick to the heterosexual.

Dick Carnall: India was a land of opportunity for all kinds. The gays created a new identity for themselves and found fulfilment in that distant land.

Parleela: Forster gives insights about England.

Dick Carnall: Not my scene. My parents were working class. I was no choirboy, nor did I go to a boarding school. You might say I'm not quite English!

PARLEELA: You people do change, howsoever slowly. Once, an Indian schoolboy writing Salman Rushdie-type English would have had a *Wren and Martin* thrown at him. Now you reward the Rushdies.

DICK CARNALL: We feel responsible for the Midnight's Mongrels.

PARLEELA: You produced them!

DICK CARNALL: Protected them from their own wicked language and literature.

PARLEELA: Indian mongrels are happy to be mongrels. But you people are unhappy with your food, your women, your nation, your arts, your sciences, your special relationship, your identity, your language.

DICK CARNALL: We are fascinated by Indian English. A travel writer quotes an Indian: "First going God, Puja doing." Afterwards Scotch whisky and German beer drinking..."

PARLEELA: Your travel writers manufacture these since their English readers love Indian English, just as they love Indian food.

DICK CARNALL: That is now. During the days of the Empire, we disliked Indian food and Hinglish to justify our rule. I have no trace of racism in me. I am ready to mix with you.

Parleela: I know what you mean by mixing!

CHAPTER FIVE

Tantric Sex
MP's OFFICE

PARLEELA: You can't go on gulping down glass after glass. Time to work. Whatever you have on your mind, please dictate.

DICK CARNALL: Your sacred *Kama Sutra* is on my mind.

PARLEELA: Reading *Kama Sutra* in Westminster! Like reading *Lolita* in Tehran!

DICK CARNALL: Communism is buried; Capitalism is gasping but Eroticism marches on!

PARLEELA: The only "ism" in harmony with the human nature!

DICK CARNALL: I can't bear those who lie back and think of England!

PARLEELA: I think of you!

DICK CARNALL: Some young English women want to break the tradition. A woman in my constituency wants Tantric Sex to be introduced in the university syllabus. She commends it as a tool of social engineering. She says it will breed satisfied and governable citizens.

PARLEELA: You asked her to give a demonstration!

DICK CARNALL: I want you to demonstrate.

PARLEELA: I was not trained in Tantric Sex.

DICK CARNALL: Forster saw India calling 'Come' through her hundred mouths. Call 'Come' through your mouth!

PARLEELA: With primitive passion!

DICK CARNALL: With colonial rage!

PARLEELA: The India of the imagination was a place to be seduced and horrified by. I fascinate and repel you!

DICK CARNALL: You capture my feeling well!

PARLEELA: Englishmen prefer words to women. When Madonna bared, you people discussed for days the usage of the word "embonpoint". It was comic! Only the American-owned *Sun* calls boobs boobs!

DICK CARNALL: What one says is very important.

PARLEELA: That is the measure of your interest in women!

DICK CARNALL: We prefer euphuism and euphemism.

PARLEELA: A legacy of the Victorian age!

DICK CARNALL: In that age, your sexuality would have been wasted.

PARLEELA: Its full potential remains untapped even today.

DICK CARNALL: Queen Victoria would have frowned upon you for not wearing underwear!

PARLEELA: You put your women into 37 pounds of constricting clothing and you feel outraged by the Muslim woman covering her face! Christian female minds and bodies were corseted at puberty. You drove your women mad by repression. Consigned the demented women to the attic! Even the piano's legs were not left uncovered!

DICK CARNALL: I will uncover yours.

PARLEELA: My legs are uncovered.

DICK CARNALL: I take you to the Saint of Underwear. M&S.

PARLEELA: You will take me nowhere. Reluctant imperialists. Reluctant lovers!

DICK CARNALL: The idea of contact between a man and woman was foreign to us. Physical love was brought to us in the 19th century by the waltzing continentals. It caused a national uproar. Our journals condemned "yielding forms, hot breaths, entwined limbs and inflamed spirit". They screamed: "Waltzing is sinning."

PARLEELA: Now sinning is waltzing.

DICK CARNALL: Then in villages, even couples married for 50 years could not hold hands in public. Elderly ladies kept an eye on them and gossiped.

PARLEELA: England has come far!

DICK CARNALL: Then we were shocked by the immoral Indian classics. The profane lovers marrying in *Shakuntala* with the "desire of amorous embraces".

PARLEELA: Now your novels are F-word compendiums.

DICK CARNAL: The literary novelists serve pornography.

PARLEELA: Under the pretext of portraying seedy Thatcherite Britain.

DICK CARNALL: BBC teaches sex to Americans. When *Coupling* was shown in America, their panting critics said the British TV programme "pushed the envelope".

PARLEELA: American TV has less sex, American life has more.

DICK CARNALL: The English make up through virtual reality.

PARLEELA: I wish *you would* get real.

DICK CARNALL: I am more Latin than English.

PARLEELA: I thought you were as English as God.

DICK CARNALL: Is that how you feel when we communicate flesh-to-flesh?

PARLEELA: Don't give yourself airs. You are a perfect English gentleman!

DICK CARNALL: Are you, like Doris Day, provoking me?

PARLEELA: It's supposed to be a compliment.

DICK CARNALL: I'm the author of *Ruling Passions.*

PARLEELA: How can you rule over passion?

DICK CARNALL: Passion rules over me as I rule over you. I'm here to possess my patrimony.

PARLEELA: In your drunken haze, you can't see me. You can't remember what you called me for. Your Prime Minister wants a brief on the Indian Prime Minister. And as your researcher, I must work on it.

DICK CARNALL: Let's work. I work on you. You work on me!

PARLEELA: No. Let's Google.

DICK CARNALL: I get excited when you say, let's.

Google! The world sleeps while we Google.

PARLEELA: Silent night.

DICK CARNALL: Make it a panting night.

PARLEELA: I thought you English liked silence. India was hated for its noises. Forster lamented, "There is no silence in the East."

DICK CARNALL: We found the noises of India unbearable. A British Captain wrote a poem *Noise at Night*:

What melancholy cries the silence break!

Do Ditchers only go to bed to wake?

What Imp nocturnal gathers from afar

The amorous cats of every vile bazaar?

I leap from bed in horror and affright,

Thinking all Bedlam broken loose tonight.

One like a furious tiger loudly growls,

Another like a beaten urchin howls.

Nor is this all, for troops of mice and rats.

Squeak out a shrill concerto to the cats,

Bothering me more beneath the shades of night

Than fifty Boxwallahs by morning light.

PARLEELA: Where did you learn that one?

DICK CARNALL: My mother said she used to recite it as a schoolgirl. Imperial memory! May 24 was Empire Day. It meant an extra holiday.

PARLEELA: The Empire now means only "Carry on up the Khyber!"

DICK CARNALL: The monarch issues the annual Commonwealth Day message!

PARLEELA: That makes no impression either at home or in the former colonies. Do I make an impression on you?

DICK CARNALL: Terrific! I love the way you pant and want! The way you moan and cry! You give yourself up as no sane woman would!

PARLEELA: The East as the seductress! To be resisted or enjoyed? Naipaul's favourite liaison is between a white male and a dark-skinned backward class woman with coarse tribal features and terrible rough voice. Emblematic of the imperial encounter!

DICK CARNALL: A novelist trying to be a diagnostician of society!

PARLEELA: Naipaul must have read the novel *Samskara* in which the high-caste hero mates with a low-caste prostitute.

DICK CARNALL: In your caste system, I am from Mars, you are from Venus.

PARLEELA: There you go. The imperial trick of feminising the one you wish to control and dominate. You did it to India. America does it to Europe.

DICK CARNALL: You are my Oriental fantasy!

PARLEELA: You fear the Orient, the female, the dark seductive force. You are stricken with Christian guilt.

DICK CARNALL: Deliver me of my guilt through our union. I dump the Bible. Reconvert to paganism.

PARLEELA: You will have to worship goddesses.

DICK CARNALL: I atone for calling Aphrodite a whore.

PARLEELA: In the latest census some Britishers call themselves "Goddess-worshipper".

DICK CARNALL: Let me enter your temple as a supplicant! I feel detached from my distant spiritual abode. I seek a home in you. You, the embodiment of the sensual India.

PARLEELA: Why do you keep bringing in India? I am a person not a territory!

DICK CARNALL: My imperial memory mixes with colonial desire. Act II, Scene I: My ruling passion rises, demands subjugation... submission... sublimation. You love me and you hate me. Say it in the same breath. Go on, say it!

PARLEELA: I freeze, I burn.

DICK CARNALL: Let me warm the cockles of your Anglophilic heart.

PARLEELA: You suffer from Indophilia.

DICK CARNALL: My bittersweet chocolate, *glykypikron!*

PARLEELA: I actualise your fantasy but I can't live your dream. I am a post-colonial girl, post-colonial and post-modern at the same time.

DICK CARNALL: We will have a post-colonial relationship!

PARLEELA: You talk like an imperial historian!

DICK CARNALL: You talk like a female multi-cultural studies professor!

PARLEELA: I am not a depository for your desires. I will not be a recipient. I am a woman of substance, not an empty vessel.

DICK CARNALL: Half-empty!

PARLEELA: Have you been to India?

DICK CARNALL: India is in my genes. My father and grandfather were there. My great grandfather served in north-eastern jungles. I discovered lost cousins in India.

PARLEELA: Their fathers were fathered in secrecy!

DICK CARNALL: The fathers ran away from their children because they could not see themselves into the faces of their children. My grandfather's diary reveals seven children whose births went unrecorded. I have cousins in Rhodesia and Malaya too.

PARLEELA: Quite an extended family!

DICK CARNALL: My grandfather had seven children. My grandmother, who didn't join him in India, had her own private tally. Though in those days, it was not that easy.

PARLEELA: Leave your past. Talk of our future!

DICK CARNALL: Lend me your delicious ear! *One, two, three, four, five, six, seven. All good men go to heaven.* I'll never be the Prime Minister. I don't have to remain married. It's all over. *Finito.* I am no husband. Who am I?

PARLEELA: A macro-molecule.

DICK CARNALL: The Right Honourable Robert Crook called me bastard in the Tea Room.

PARLEELA: He envies you because of me.

DICK CARNALL: I am Nobody. I will never be the Prime Minister. Why am I here?

PARLEELA: To atone for your past sins.

DICK CARNALL: Then why am I being made to commit more?

PARLEELA: Because life must go on, sustained by sin.

DICK CARNALL: I know why I am here! To enjoy your golden apples! This room is my Garden of Eden and I am about to fall!

PARLEELA: Your mind is overheated. Your passion has cooled. You have fallen.

DICK CARNALL: Be my Queen and command: Arise!

PARLEELA: You cannot be aroused.

DICK CARNALL: My Black Beauty, boost my ego, I beseech you! Fill my cup. I fill yours. Here you are!

(Glasses tinkle)

PARLEELA: Don't talk. In Italy, in Latin America, in India, nothing is said before or after. In this island, all said and done, more is said than done.

DICK CARNALL: We are English! "That's not done" is our favourite phrase. We define ourselves by what we aren't and what we don't do.

PARLEELA: You don't eat garlic.

DICK CARNALL: I taste your mouth and know you are not English.

PARLEELA: Stop. Remember Lord Profumo!

DICK CARNALL: Who does not remember the Profumo Affair? That War Minister and Christine Keeler could have ended the cold war years before it ended. Capt. Ivanov, who was sleeping with Christine Keeler, was our man. The tabloids spoilt it all.

PARLEELA: Almost brought the British cabinet down.

DICK CARNALL: I play the osteopath. You play Christine and run naked around the swimming pool!

PARLEELA: Those were exciting times. Cold War fears stoked the fires of sex.

DICK CARNALL: The end of the Cold War did not dampen desire. An English minister sucked a Spanish woman's toe!

PARLEELA: John Major had to unleash the Back-to-Basics campaign.

DICK CARNALL: It sparked a rebellion. The Shadow Arts Secretary declared he could not do his job unless he had sexual flexibility.

PARLEELA: Well, he paid for that flexibility!

DICK CARNALL: He remained an MP. The people forgive and forget.

PARLEELA: Wait till you are exposed!

DICK CARNALL: If we are outed, I will earn more from TV interviews. So will you!

PARLEELA: Toe-sucking may cost you ministership.

Your leader will throw you out.

DICK CARNALL: You are my leader. I accept your whip.

Make my pain your pleasure!

PARLEELA: Don't be unconventional. The MP who misused a polythene bag was found dead.

DICK CARNALL: You are my shepherd; I am your sheep. You are my mistress, I bleat.

PARLEELA: Will love-in lead to live-in?

DICK CARNALL: A difficult question in the Age of Uncertainty.

PARLEELA: Will you take me as your legally wedded wife?

DICK CARNALL: I will just take you.

PARLEELA: As what?

DICK CARNALL: Forever and forever, we will remain friends, intimate friends.

PARLEELA: Only friends!

DICK CARNALL: All friends cannot be spouses. All spouses cannot be friends.

PARLEELA: Thank you for your friendship!

DICK CARNALL: The Thais are wise. Most Thai Members of Parliament have a *mianoi*, minor wife.

PARLEELA: In traditional South India, the husband has a "big house" and a "small house".

DICK CARNALL: Then why do you keep asking me, "As what?"

PARLEELA: I am tired of your lip service.

DICK CARNALL: I give you non-verbal cues.

PARLEELA: Like what? Your flushed face? Red eyes? Fast breathing? Grasping hands? Darting tongue? How long are we to play this game?

DICK CARNALL: The game has hardly begun.

PARLEELA: If you are glad, I will be blunt. When do you wish to dispose of your loyal wife? You need her only during the election campaign. That is all that the long-suffering Tory wives are good for.

DICK CARNALL: She is no wife. She hasn't been a real wife for years. But I can't dump her. And I can't live without you. She is the cake and you are the icing.

PARLEELA: Then where is our future that you talk of when you are drunk? We have no future. This Disunited Kingdom has no future!

DICK CARNALL: Grab the present. Make the most of it. Together, you and me.

PARLEELA: Who are we? You tell me!

DICK CARNALL: I am you and you are me. We are entwined. In your beginning is my end. We are one. We are us. We are matter, we are anti-matter. We are here, we were there. We are. We have happened. We are the present. We are the past. We are the reality. We are an illusion. Let's move towards fusion.

PARLEELA: Don't talk like the Indian logician debating whether the milk is in the glass or the glass is in the milk.

DICK CARNALL: The contained mirrors the container. I am a Quantum Man. I am alive and I am dead. I am dead and I am alive. Dead or alive, I am ready to unite with you.

PARLEELA: Unity for a moment, or for a millennium?

DICK CARNALL: This moment is our life and it is like a lifetime. We are having the time of our life!

PARLEELA: Till dawn.

DICK CARNALL: Nothing is perennial. Not even the perennial philosophy. Perceptions change. Positions change.

PARLEELA: Mobility is modernity.

DICK CARNALL: Pain is pleasure. Stability is motion. Flux is stationary. You are Me. I am You.

PARLEELA: Words, words, words. They butter no parsnip. You keep repeating what you want. You never ask me what I want. Male pig!

DICK CARNALL: Don't be an Englishwoman.

PARLEELA: She has freed herself. No longer does she write under a man's name.

DICK CARNALL: Now men write under women's names to sell their books.

PARLEELA: What's wrong with the Englishwoman?

DICK CARNALL: She sold her feminity for feminism, sold her heart to preserve the body. She is aggressive.

PARLEELA: She wasn't always like this. In your old paintings, the feminine figure is reclining, waiting.

DICK CARNALL: Today's Englishwoman stands clawing. So unlike the gentle and submissive woman of the East.

PARLEELA: I will not be passive and spoken for. I can speak. I will not submit. You violate me by proxy.

DICK CARNALL: Not by proxy.

PARLEELA: You want me for my loyalty, not love. I'm no Phuong who can't love. You can't possess me by throwing a trinket at me. I have attributes.

DICK CARNALL: And physical assets.

PARLEELA: Don't reify me. Abstract me into a symbol!

DICK CARNALL: In temper, you look more beautiful. Your cheeks are red. Your eyes are dark. You are in heat.

PARLEELA: You are cold!

DICK CARNALL: I want to discover you. We discovered India.

PARLEELA: That was a discovery of Error!

DICK CARNALL: You are no Error. You are my religion. I want to reach where no one has gone before.

PARLEELA: Times have changed. *White Man's Way* has made me wiser. No explorer can just barge in.

DICK CARNALL: I carry the Monarch's Order to let me in. I will take you by force!

PARLEELA: You shall not.

DICK CARNALL: I am incandescent with the white heat of passion. I burn with desire! Quench my fire! You fill my cup. I fill yours!

PARLEELA: If you are thinking what I think you are thinking, stop!

DICK CARNALL: I am not thinking.

PARLEELA: But I'm thinking. I'm speaking. Can the subaltern speak? Yes, I can. Yes, I can. You will not do to me what your forefathers did to my country. Now I will do that to you.

DICK CARNALL: Let's get on then, you and me!

PARLEELA: All the way, you say.

DICK CARNALL: Comes the moment of indiscretion!

PARLEELA: At this godly hour?

DICK CARNALL: We make it an ungodly hour.

PARLEELA: You sin.

DICK CARNALL: I sin, you sin, we sin.

PARLEELA: I love your sinning self.

DICK CARNALL: Put on your dancing shoes. Dance the Dark Dancer! Dance in the dark!

PARLEELA: I see a serpent!

DICK CARNALL: It is about to bite you.

PARLEELA: Put out the light.

DICK CARNALL: Put out the light.

PARLEELA: And put out the light!

DICK CARNALL: Thank you.

PARLEELA: Thank you!

DICK CARNALL: Where are you?

PARLEELA: Seek and thou shalt find!

(Sound of Carnall rushing towards Parleela, in the dark, stumbling and making a flower vase fall)

CHAPTER SIX

Love, Actually
MP's OFFICE

PARLEELA: What is love? Even literature does not make me wiser. In fact, it confuses me further!

DICK CARNALL: Love in literature keeps changing by the age.

PARLEELA: You are right. Does Jane Austen write about love or about selecting a good mate? Her world is full of discriminating females. Can such creatures really love?

DICK CARNALL: Reproduction and survival were the issues in the England of Jane Austen. Read *Madam Bovary's Ovaries* for a Drawinian look at literature. The author calls Jane Austen "the poet laureate of female choice".

PARLEELA: Irrelevant in the England of Hanif Kureishi and Martin Amis! The modern novel is not an affair of the heart.

DICK CARNALL: It can do without a hero! Women do it to themselves.

PARLEELA: Mr. Darcy has no selling points now. Jemima will never date him.

DICK CARNALL: Parleela, your intercourse with literature is obsessive. I must compete with a book! Don't romanticise. Be a realist.

PARLEELA: Love has got degraded by pornography.

DICK CARNALL: "Sclerotic Eros", said Saul Bellow.

PARLEELA: Love in the time of the Mad Cow Disease! The literary love landscape is bleak. Literature has lost love.

DICK CARNALL: Literature and life are different universes.

PARLEELA: Literature is life.

DICK CARNALL: Life is not literature. Mix them and you will suffer.

PARLEELA: Keep them apart and you will never enjoy life. I want to live literature.

DICK CARNALL: Millions read books but live normal lives.

PARLEELA: You don't take books seriously.

DICK CARNALL: Literature is literature, life is life. Shakespeare ran a theatre company. T S Eliot worked in Lloyds Bank. Graham Greene worked for the Foreign Office. So did Sheridan. Mann was an insurance agent. Sassoon was a soldier. Whitman was a nurse in the civil war. A top American poet is a marketing manager. Compartmentalise and live!

PARLEELA: How dreadful!

DICK CARNALL: Poets win prizes, keep accounts, file bank statements, fight elections, run smear campaigns, read on the radio, flirt with friends' wives, organise abortions, make investments and draw dividends.

PARLEELA: I know what you are trying to say. No philosopher endures the toothache patiently!

DICK CARNALL: Authors hire agents.

PARLEELA: Theologians do TV talk shows!

DICK CARNALL: A university librarian thinks of sex.

PARLEELA: A priest does it.

DICK CARNALL: Even solipsists look both ways before crossing a street.

PARLEELA: Post-modernists submit their appendicitis to a surgeon, not to a semiotician.

DICK CARNALL: A feminist weeps.

PARLEELA: How sad!

DICK CARNALL: Give up your romantic notion of a poet.

PARLEELA: A poet can't drive.

DICK CARNALL: A poet shouldn't drive, as Martin Amis said.

PARLEELA: I love the Romantics.

DICK CARNALL: Romantic poetry has an element of artifice. Keats said a poet is not itself, it has no self, it's everything and nothing. A poet is the most impoetical of anything in existence because he has no identity.

PARLEELA: Ethereal!

DICK CARNALL: Legislators of mankind, my foot! We MPs are the legislators. Stop dreaming of a poet. Start loving me.

PARLEELA: Why can't life be literature?

DICK CARNALL: Life gets more exciting than literature when we two are alone at night.

PARLEELA: Where are love-lorn poets? Where is love poetry?

DICK CARNALL: On Valentine cards.

PARLEELA: Where are true lovers?

DICK CARNALL: Were they ever there? The past just appears romantic. Lovers do not die of love. They die of death. Parleela, you live in a world of fantasy. Romantic novels set your heart on fire. Books can burn.

PARLEELA: If I avoid fire, I cannot be alive.

DICK CARNALL: Then come, play with fire!

PARLEELA: Reading ruins but I wanted to be ruined.

DICK CARNALL: Books put ideas into your head!

PARLEELA: *Lady Chatterley's Lover* awakened my body. Made me pine for a literary version of life.

DICK CARNALL: That's why for long we kept women away from books.

PARLEELA: You used the Book to convert the savages.

DICK CARNALL: We used poets as cannon balls to suppress mischief in India!

PARLEELA: I lapped up English literature. Failed to see it as a tool of cultural imperialism. Indians saw an Englishman in the image of Shakespeare or Shelley and not as Col. D'yer! The use and abuse of literature!

DICK CARNALL: We cursed India with a derivative discourse. We saw to it that Indians could never write a book of their own.

PARLEELA: Enslavement of the mind was the price for the liberation of the body!

DICK CARNALL: Books awaken women and transform politics. Look what *Lady Chatterley's Lover* did to you! A bearded Jew wrote a book in the British Museum and look what it did to the world!

PARLEELA: I want to live a literary version of life.

DICK CARNALL: To internalise a borrowed emotion, catalyse passion.

PARLEELA: There is much to be said about an adulterous relationship and adulterous writers!

DICK CARNALL: Adultery is an idea that has become immensely popular.

PARLEELA: D H Lawrence glamorised it; Graham Greene elevated it to the spiritual level. It cannot be put back into the bottle.

DICK CARNALL: Adultery is supported by the weight of literature. Without adultery, British publishing will go bankrupt; the theatre district will close down. Hollywood will make no money. The Anglosphere will be in chaos.

PARLEELA: Adultery gets bad press but it is so tempting. It is a font of creativity. Literature owes a debt to adultery.

DICK CARNALL: Life too.

PARLEELA: Adultery in literature exercises immense power and influence. From the printed page, it transformed me. But for *Anna Karenina*, I would have been Sita or Gita.

DICK CARNALL: It made you Anna of the Tropics.

PARLEELA: *Anna Karenina* saved the novel from narrative impotence.

DICK CARNALL: It seduced millions.

PARLEELA: I was one.

DICK CARNALL: You tried to be a woman of the book.

PARLEELA: Graham Greene turned me into Sarah Miles. I memorised the lines about God and Love. Went to the church to make the promise and then to his flat to break the promise.

DICK CARNALL: Greene was not writing a self-help guide!

PARLEELA: Adultery is more than what the upper-class England thinks. More than a fashionable after-dinner party game. It epitomises the serial logic.

DICK CARNALL: It's a rebellion against faith.

PARLEELA: No. Adultery has a spiritual dimension. God is the third party in the Sarah-Maurice affair. Graham Greene saw the Church as a shrine to adultery. Like his bedsit, 14 North Side Clapham Common.

DICK CARNALL: Why hesitate then?

PARLEELA: Because I'm still not entirely comfortable with sin.

DICK CARNALL: Sin leads to salvation. In order to repent, we must sin.

PARLEELA: I know that the sinner has God constantly in front of him. I think of God only when I'm being wicked.

DICK CARNALL: Sin in order to be human! God doesn't want competition.

PARLEELA: Life without literature will be mundane. We imitate responses. Enact what we read. Relate the literary experience to personal life. Literature nurtures. Nurture overwrites nature. Just as we learn to read, we learn to feel. We feel nothing on our own. We don't even know what can be felt unless we read it or see it in a play or a film. Poets, painters, dramatists, and novelists. They make us feel. They make us free. They make us fantasise.

DICK CARNALL: The connection between life and literature or literature and life is complicated. Each explicates the other.

PARLEELA: It's the ultimate experience.

DICK CARNALL: The most adventurous boundary-crossing.

PARLEELA: The defining event of the Great 19th century bourgeois novel.

DICK CARNALL: The literary uses of ****ing!

PARLEELA: I catch myself acting out fiction.

DICK CARNALL: Act out the *Kama Sutra*! Exteriorise that piece of literature.

PARLEELA: To be a fictional heroine, I rebelled against morality.

DICK CARNALL: We enact an immorality play!

PARLEELA: Charlotte Bronte dipped her pen into passion.

DICK CARNALL: I'm ready to dip my pen.

PARLEELA: Ideas and emotions, packaged attractively, are easily planted. We pick up an idea, like a shampoo bottle.

DICK CARNALL: That was the idea of imperialism. That's how we turn savages into nobles.

PARLEELA: Jane Eyre views St John's mission to improve the people of India to be as misguided and hubristic as his attempts to improve Jane.

DICK CARNALL: The feminist critique of Empire comes from an obsession with gender inequalities. Women could not be trusted. Fictive desire threatened our social order. James Joyce showed how a woman could work herself up.

PARLEELA: He was fine with the men using magazines to work themselves up!

DICK CARNALL: Magazines are not needed in the internet age!

PARLEELA: The English novel taught me to pine for a tall, dark, and handsome Prince. He lived in the book.

DICK CARNALL: Abuse of literacy! What did you read?

PARLEELA: The classics. Mills and Boon.

DICK CARNALL: Cheap romantic fiction sells in India!

PARLEELA: Because of arranged marriages and because of the absence of desire and fulfilment.

DICK CARNALL: I am ready to fulfil your desire!

PARLEELA: Fiction transforms you. Makes you want to be someone else. You want to exist in a character. Nothing ordinary suits you. You want to be part of a grand narrative.

DICK CARNALL: It happens even to nations. We, the English, had a grand narrative once.

PARLEELA: India too, some centuries ago!

DICK CARNALL: Israel has imagined a grand narrative. It can't accept a routine existence. It will never have peace.

PARLEELA: I'll never have peace. I want perpetual excitement!

DICK CARNALL: Be with me and you shall have it!

PARLEELA: What if my life fails to mimic literature? I fear that my life will fall short of literature.

DICK CARNALL: The literature that falls short of life displeases critic.

PARLEELA: Can a professor of literature love? He may critique love while making love! What about a philosopher?

DICK CARNALL: Even logical positivists are capable of love, A J Ayer believed.

PARLEELA: The male gynecologist? While running his hands over the breasts, he thinks of nerves, cells, tissues, veins. Can he see a pink lotus flowering?

DICK CARNALL: A man of science will view Raquel Welch as an imperfect human body.

PARLEELA: The poet believes he alone can imagine a woman. He can't imagine others doing it! Auden speculates when a politician dreams about his sweetheart, does he multiply her face into a crowd? In *Heavy Date,* Auden asks: *"Does he try to buy her, / Is the kissing loud?"*

DICK CARNALL: Don't divide up a man like that.

PARLEELA: An economist thinks of gross output while removing her underwear. A strategist thinks of the Indian Ocean while undressing his love.

DICK CARNALL: Only a prostitute is capable of *real* true love. Purest.

PARLEELA: Votes with the lips against the market!

DICK CARNALL: Anyone can make a virtuous woman fall in love. It's damn hard with a professional. He who makes a prostitute fall in love is the ultimate lover! That's why films are made of such stuff!

PARLEELA: Do I just parrot a line from a book? Or do I really feel? How does an actress love in life?

DICK CARNALL: With imitable passion.

PARLEELA: She is a trained lover.

DICK CARNALL: Like a trained housewife or a trained cook.

PARLEELA: An actress passes screen tests before falling in love. With all that voice training, does *she* speak or shut her eyes and say nothing? Does her face have the expression that it had before?

DICK CARNALL: In this scene, she is without the Director. She improvises.

PARLEELA: Surely her screen lines come gushing to her lips. Can an actress ever fall in love? How does she know that this time, she *is* in love? That it is the *Real Thing?*

DICK CARNALL: We are all actors. Shakespeare knew that.

PARLEELA: He was right. After all, situations are standard. Plots are fixed. The routine is rehearsed. We fall in love. We are betrayed. We part. We regret. We love again. We fall in a rut. We recover. We repeat.

DICK CARNALL: Nothing is original. Every TV serial-watcher knows.

PARLEELA: TV viewers can never be lovers with genuine feelings!

DICK CARNALL: The media mediates.

PARLEELA: The serial watchers have nothing of their own to say or feel. They borrow emotions. They parrot. They repeat themselves like a broken record. They mimic!

DICK CARNALL: Let's mimic.

PARLEELA: We are doing it. I feel whatever I feel is just an echo. It has been felt before. Nothing is original. Nothing is authentic. Nothing is spontaneous.

DICK CARNALL: You say scholarly things. I guess you use ideas like men use Viagra.

PARLEELA: I want to play-act.

DICK CARNALL: Love begins with play-acting. Drama makes you understand life. We all dramatise. I lie for love!

PARLEELA: Can you die for love?

DICK CARNALL: If the script so requires.

PARLEELA: Love continues after you die, says an insurance ad.

DICK CARNALL: Love continues while we live tonight.

PARLEELA: What is this thing called love? O tell me the truth about love!

DICK CARNALL: Love works in mysterious ways.

PARLEELA: In silence or with words?

DICK CARNALL: If Love were inarticulate, what would writers do?

PARLEELA: Love can't be both sightless and speechless.

DICK CARNALL: Words won't help if we speak different languages.

PARLEELA: Your four-letter word is universal!

DICK CARNALL: Let no words come between us. Let no words delay action.

PARLEELA: Love is divine!

DICK CARNALL: Let's partake divinity!

PARLEELA: Love is unrealisable.

DICK CARNALL: True love happens between incompatibles.

PARLEELA: Like our East-West affair.

DICK CARNALL: Incompatibility, like life, tests love.

PARLEELA: Rich-girl-poor-boy love stories are exciting.

DICK CARNALL: Diana proved that love is not made in a palace.

PARLEELA: An unclean bed in a tawdry hotel room cradles true love.

DICK CARNALL: Stealth enhances the thrill!

PARLEELA: We love only once. Then on it is all self-delusions.

DICK CARNALL: I give repeat performances.

PARLEELA: What is true love? Unconditional love. Love that comes gushing with all its destructive force. Love that lives on after I'm gone.

DICK CARNALL: Only in books.

PARLEELA: I found my first love among books.

DICK CARNALL: Under the covers!

PARLEELA: Between the sheets!

DICK CARNALL: In the bedroom?

PARLEELA: No. In a library! A quiet place.

DICK CARNALL: Like a grave.

PARLEELA: "A man's library is a kind of harem", said Emerson.

DICK CARNALL: Library is an erotic place. Larkin got dirty thoughts there.

PARLEELA: It was in a library that I first blushed.

DICK CARNALL: Not in a garden, like a Bollywood heroine!

PARLEELA: Behind the stacks, "love" came whispering. In the college library, our lips were locked.

DICK CARNALL: Which was rather late. English girls begin in school.

PARLEELA: Love, born in a library and nourished by metre and metaphors!

DICK CARNALL: Flowered in Westminster!

PARLEELA: Was there no love before the Renaissance?

DICK CARNALL: Dating love is difficult.

PARLEELA: I can date my love to the precise moment in human history.

DICK CARNALL: You are funny. You are smart. You are thoughtful. You are beautiful. You are delightful. You are sweet. You are delectable. Is there a special school for Indian women? You read, you write, you joke, you cook, you suck, you ****. Shall I go on?

PARLEELA: If I splash cold water on your face, you might talk sense.

DICK CARNALL: If I splash hot chocolate on your body, it might make love.

DICK CARNALL: Love may erupt or love may creep but it always makes you weep.

PARLEELA: Love is not love if it subsides without a scar.

DICK CARNALL: Love is not love if not recorded in history. A lover built a monument so that his love is remembered for centuries.

PARLEELA: Love hurts.

DICK CARNALL: Lust heals.

PARLEELA: Love is a bedfellow of unhappiness!

DICK CARNALL: Love me and be happy!

PARLEELA: Love makes a tormented, tortured manic genius desirable.

DICK CARNALL: Don't go for a mad man. Come to me!

PARLEELA: Alas, my love is not blind. I can't fall in love over a dish of onions.

DICK CARNALL: A touch of hair is enough for a Graham Greene hero! Touch me with your black hair!

PARLEELA: My love stands below a spiral staircase and shouts Parleela!

DICK CARNALL: You are not Hollywood's Stella!

PARLEELA: I'm looking for a soul mate.

DICK CARNALL: I'm looking for a body mate!

PARLEELA: In England everyone is looking for that.

DICK CARNALL: The search peaks on Friday nights!

PARLEELA: Is love a matter of chance or choice?

DICK CARNALL: The compulsion of addiction.

PARLEELA: Are lovers born?

DICK CARNALL: Made by hallucination.

PARLEELA: Can one fall in love without assuming a false self?

DICK CARNALL: True love is related to the inner self.

PARLEELA: I want love but what do I want out of love?

DICK CARNALL: Stop talking and start loving!

PARLEELA: Hyperbole dampens! Metaphors burn out! Feelings go sour! Passion turns monotonous! Is this the way love goes?

DICK CARNALL: Nothing lasts. Not even love.

PARLEELA: What do I pick in the supermarket of love? Where do I begin?

DICK CARNALL: In your beginning is your end.

PARLEELA: Do I target the brain or the stomach?

DICK CARNALL: Go lower to feel the erotic spark!

PARLEELA: In love, tinsel looks better than gold!

DICK CARNALL: Flaubert rated the poetry of tinsel greater because it is sadder.

PARLEELA: Politicians are hard nuts but I see that you fantasise!

DICK CARNALL: "All fantasies are good in matters of love": Charles Fourier.

PARLEELA: Is fantasy a matter of the brain or heart?

DICK CARNALL: Heart is a blood pump that you cannot see. See the pump that feels the blood, this instrument of interconnectedness.

PARLEELA: Delve deep or taste not...I am not for a quickie!

DICK CARNALL: Life is hectic. We must have love on the run.

PARLEELA: Love without thought is lust.

DICK CARNALL: Brain is the worst part to have sex on.

PARLEELA: Love takes time. Love lasts.

DICK CARNALL: A "noble orgy" outlasts love.

PARLEELA: Don't talk of lust. Talk of love.

DICK CARNALL: Love may last but, in the end, quotidian rules.

PARLEELA: Love liberates.

DICK CARNALL: Lust shoots through barriers, breaches boundaries. Frees you of shackles and shame. The Free World fights puritanical tyranny, repeals obscenity laws, encourages minority tastes in sex. I love lust.

PARLEELA: Rather obvious from your video collection. Such videos ruin the love lives of Indian husbands in England.

DICK CARNALL: These liberate their wives. Nothing is perverse in love. Love and lust go together like second and first. Two chapters of the same book. Petals of the same flower. Lust is a genuine item, hard to counterfeit and hard to intellectualise.

PARLEELA: Scholars do.

DICK CARNALL: Lust is love that gets a bad press. Don't fight it.

PARLEELA: Hard to fight. Hard to hide. I know it.

DICK CARNALL: Lust rules life and literature.

PARLEELA: Writers don't just reflect the world. They help make it.

DICK CARNALL: We politicians remake the world!

PARLEELA: You politicians mess up the world.

DICK CARNALL: It is because of us and not because of the poets that the world is making progress.

PARLEELA: Progress is an illusion. The world will progress to extinction. There will be no golden dawn. Truth is always awaited, always round the corner, never found. String Theorists promise an elegant universe. Scientists chase fusion, the nuclear *Kamdhenu.* They say one thing today and the opposite tomorrow. Today's breakthroughs are tomorrow's hoaxes. Designer drugs are hailed only to be discarded. Black holes go into a black hole. Where is Literary Theory today? Moral philosophers cause confusion. Ideas come into fashion and fade out. Some are killed by their originators.

DICK CARNALL: You're drunk! Fill my glass.

(Sound of pouring and tinkling glasses)

PARLEELA: Here you go. I feel dizzy. I'm ready to fall.

DICK CARNALL: We will. We will. We will.

PARLEELA: I say what you say! *Five, six, seven, we go to heaven!* I lust.

DICK CARNALL: Give it a free play! Controlling lust is undesirable. It gives you pride of resistance. Don't try to be virtuous.

PARLEELA: Down with virtue!

DICK CARNALL: Up with vice!

PARLEELA: Virtue, modesty, chastity! All erotic values! Not moral values! Their purpose is to make women attractive, not to God but to men. Old Bollywood movies showed drunkard heroes but school-teacher heroines!

DICK CARNALL: You have a point or rather two points!

PARLEELA: Women have.

DICK CARNALL: Enough talk of sin. Let's sin! God needs sinners to carry on his business. That's why I sin, sin with country lasses and girls who wear glasses.

PARLEELA: You have an escebtric gene! Is there love that does not ask why?

DICK CARNALL: Let's do and die! Be a butterfly!

PARLEELA: It'll be glorious to die for love.

DICK CARNALL: The God of Sex and the God of Death are the same in many traditions!

PARLEELA: Don't talk of either if you want to be Prime Minister.

DICK CARNALL: I am done with politics. Undo me!

PARLEELA: Love has undone so many! See the tragic plays!

DICK CARNALL: Drama ends; life must be lived on. Life may be drama but drama is not life.

PARLEELA: Drama giveth life.

DICK CARNALL: It taketh away life when life gets dramatised. Life spurts through induction of literature but then ebbs away.

PARLEELA: That death is glorious.

DICK CARNALL: Literature sucks life. Fiction hollows out its subject.

PARLEELA: I want to walk into the river, in the footsteps of Virginia Woolf. I want to be a Sylvia Plath. Oh, to end life loving a poet-lover! Or hating!

DICK CARNALL: Your death-romanticism puts you in a state of excitement. A chemical reaction is on.

PARLEELA: Are we real?

DICK CARNALL: If we are shot at this moment, it will be a natural film. *Cine-verite*. Not *reel* life. Real life!

PARLEELA: I will get a knife. Let's introduce a crime of passion!

DICK CARNALL: You can't kill me twice.

PARLEELA: I think of death when I read a novel pulsating with life. The English novel corralled me into a foreign fantasy!

DICK CARNALL: Stop fantasising! We are real.

PARLEELA: We have strayed far. Tonight I want your final answer. It is a matter of my life and death. How long will our secret tryst last? We may soon be discovered!

DICK CARNALL: Good God! Don't you ever fantasise about selling our story to a tabloid.

PARLEELA: Bed-and-tell!

DICK CARNALL: Has someone tried to tempt you?

PARLEELA: Imagine the fictional version of our affair! It will capture the excitement, the erotic tension, the danger, the secrecy, the comedy, the betrayal, all inherent in our situation.

DICK CARNALL: Don't you frighten me!

PARLEELA: How will they retell our story? How will they reinvent us? Will they garnish us for aesthetic reasons? Will our tale be beautiful or seedy? Who will I be? The huntress or the hunted? Will they make me capable of suffering? What end will I meet? Of a mistress murdered by her employer MP!

DICK CARNALL: How dreadful!

PARLEELA: Will they make a cheap docudrama out of us? Will we feature in a breakfast sex show? Or be immortalised in a political comedy?

DICK CARNALL: They could invite me to play myself!

PARLEELA: Will they superimpose an internal conflict on you? Will you be modelled on Graham Greene battling to reconcile sex and morality or on Malcolm Muggeridge, free of such conflict? Or on an 18th century philanderer-politician? They may inject Catholicism into our affair.

DICK CARNALL: Old hat! They will make it topical. Give it a modern twist! Give it a surreal touch because we are Britain's moderns.

PARLEELA: A contemporary debate will be woven into our tale. The Conservatives and Liberals will fight over us!

DICK CARNALL: On the small screen we will go on and on for months! My acting fee will be more than my salary as an MP.

PARLEELA: You are money mad. Do you take cash for questions?

DICK CARNALL: No. I don't. I have no minor vices.

PARLEELA: The real you should be exposed. I want to out myself and out you! End this charade! I can bear it no more. I want peace.

DICK CARNALL: Don't get so worked up.

PARLEELA: I want to lie no more. I shall tell the truth. Live the truth. I want real drama.

DICK CARNALL: Your obsession with dramatic life is getting dangerous.

PARLEELA: I want my life to end in a flash, with a flourish, in a glorious climax, to a thunderous applause, the curtain coming down with "Bravo, Bravo".

Dıck Carnall: The Romantic Myth of the Dead Young Poet has cast a spell on you. Don't romanticise death. Death is not a miracle. It is achievable. Everyone gets it. Death is nothing. There is only drama in death!

Parleela: I crave for drama in life!

Dıck Carnall: Come. Let me take you to the terrace! Come with me.

Parleela: For what? To push me down in the darkness of the night and plant a story of suicide in the tabloids? You think my death wish is real?

Dıck Carnall: What are you saying? Have you gone mad?

Parleela: No. I don't want to die yet. Have I become an embarrassment for you? You think I will come between you and the primeministership. You can't dispose me off that easily. Not another murder in the Palace of Westminster! I am not coming to the terrace with you. I will not fall into that trap. You cannot push me down from the terrace. I court life, not death.

(The telephone rings. Parleela picks up the receiver)

Parleela: Hello!

Dıck Carnall: Who could be ringing at this hour? Why did you pick up the receiver? You are not supposed to be here. Why did you say hello? We are finished! They know I'm with a female.

(Snatches the receiver. Listens and shouts)

DICK CARNALL: You bloody racist reporter. I am working with my Research Assistant. You have no bloody business to poke your nose into my business. How does her race or colour matter? How dare you snoop on us? How dare you listen to our conversation live through a planted device? What, you are parked outside the building? You have recorded our voices and hacked our email accounts! What films we saw on the Red-Hot Channel is no bloody business of yours. No public money was involved. Your owner wants to destabilise my party's Government. That is why he assigned you this sting operation. This is not America. What do you want?

PARLEELA: (Whispering): Don't mess with the media.

DICK CARNALL (*Away from the receiver*): Keep quiet. I will deal with him. *(Into the phone)* How dare you record my conversation? It is a breach of the Official Secrets Act, a breach of my parliamentary privileges. My working relationship with my Research Assistant is of no concern of yours. What is wrong in my telling her to come to the terrace?

PARLEELA: *(Softly):* So he knows all about us!

DICK CARNALL *(Shouting)*: What compromising position? What photographs? What conversation? You think you can harm me politically? Britain is not puritanical. It never was, not even before your filthy tabloid started flooding it with the photos of Page-3 girls. Britain is a gay nation. The people like gaiety. Remember, here a top political leader bragged about seducing sisters and secretaries. Here MPs have been discovered in all kinds of compromising positions. A dead prostitute in the room could do no harm. We have a noble tradition.

PARLEELA: *(Whispering):* You are giving the media more *masala*, ammunition! Don't do that.

DICK CARNALL: Publish your bloody story and be damned. My voters would like me even more. They want their MP to be normal, one with whom they can identify. They find it easy to relate to me because I do what they all do. I am one of Them! Parleela's race will go in my favour in our multi-cultural Britain.

PARLEELA: Oh, so that was what you were banking on. On the colour of my skin. I thought you loved me.

DICK CARNALL (*Ignoring Parleela):* How dare you say that I planned to murder Parleela by taking her to the terrace? Print any such allegation and I will see to it that your newspaper is closed and your American owner arrested.

PARLEELA: What are doing? You are taking on the might of the *Half Moon* publications. Every British Prime Minister kept this media mogul in good humour. The Media Monopoly Amendment Bill was drafted by the *Half Moon* editor.

DICK CARNALL (*Shouting*): You heard me. Publish and be damned! Damn you. Go to hell!

(Bangs the telephone down)

PARLEELA: So, it is goodbye now! We did enjoy for a while. It was nice knowing you, Right Honourable Dick Carnall, MP! All good things come to an end. Nothing lasts. Goodbye!

DICK CARNALL: What? No. It is not goodbye to you.

PARLEELA: Then?

DICK CARNALL: It is goodbye to my political career.

PARLEELA: What? Are you mad!

DICK CARNALL: You are worth it! You are worth it!

PARLEELA: Don't be a fool. Your wife, your children, your constituency, career!

DICK CARNALL: Let all go to Hell!

PARLEELA: Love me, don't fear me. I was just joking. I will never expose you. I will go quietly; fade away. I will never talk to a tabloid reporter. I promise.

DICK CARNALL: My Parleela, you could never make me out! How could you? You are fed the daily diet of the tabloids. You don't hold a British politician in high esteem.

PARLEELA: If you are joking, it is a cruel joke.

DICK CARNALL: No. Today I will say what I have never said before in a somber moment. I love you!

PARLEELA: I can't take such jokes. I am traumatised.

DICK CARNALL: Why? For Heaven's sake, why?

PARLEELA: Don't ask me. You know why. I am leaving Britain. I will go to India to heal myself. I will not be here on Sunday to read any tabloid. I have had enough of Britain and of you. I can't play along anymore. This double life ends tonight. Tomorrow I will be me again.

DICK CARNALL: Why are you getting upset? I am telling the truth. Tomorrow morning, we will be free of fear. We will hold our heads high. You and me! I will address a press conference, come clean and release a public statement.

PARLEELA: A public statement about us?

DICK CARNALL: Yes, about us. About our future. You often asked me about our future. I will give you a formal answer in front of millions of TV viewers. I shall do what no British politician has done for a woman.

PARLEELA: What is that?

DICK CARNALL: I will resign from the House of Commons, divorce my wife and marry you.

PARLEELA: Me? I don't want you to sacrifice all in a fit of righteousness.

DICK CARNALL: In a fit of True Love.

PARLEELA: Oh, my darling! Don't just throw away the political capital earned over so many years.

DICK CARNALL: You are worth it!

PARLEELA: Am I? I wonder. Are you sure?

DICK CARNALL: We will soon be off to India as man and wife for our honeymoon in Goa.

PARLEELA: A honeymoon in Goa! A night in Paris! A day in Davos! And what else?

DICK CARNALL: I'm serious.

PARLEELA: I have heard it before!

DICK CARNALL: I'm dead serious. My grandfather was a tea planter in India. I spent three years there during my childhood. I want to take you there.

PARLEELA: You want to take me everywhere!

DICK CARNALL: I want to live in India. We will settle down in Darjeeling. We will grow roses, the fragrant rose, not the English rose. We will live in a bungalow with servants. We will have tea in the verandah and live happily ever after.

PARLEELA: But a few moments ago you wanted to take me to the terrace. Why?

DICK CARNALL: To show you the full moon, silly! Don't lovers in India look at the moon together?

PARLEELA: Oh, God! How horrible of me. I did great injustice to you in my mind. Imagined you wanted to push me down from the terrace and make the police register a case of suicide. You did not want me to come in the way of your becoming the Prime Minister. I thought you planned to get rid of me before a tabloid got wind of us. I have seen it happening! Forgive me. I fall on your feet to apologise.

DICK CARNALL: Fall on me!

PARLEELA: Astounding! I can't believe it. A sudden new twist in our tale!

DICK CARNALL: One Act has ended.

PARLEELA: Let the next Act begin!

DICK CARNALL: Come!

PARLEELA: Here I come! *One, two, three, four, five, six, seven/ You and I go to Heaven!*

DICK CARNALL: *We two go to Heaven!*

SECOND MP IN SECURITY PASS ROW

Sex and British Politics

Parleela and her MP friend, carrying on in the privacy of Westminster Palace, at recall an earlier event in the history of British scandals in which an India-born woman, with the House of Commons security pass, rocked the British establishment.

That *Haryana-ki-Beti*, then known as Pamella Bordes, got exposed as a secret 500-pounds-a-night call girl. In one photograph she was seen with a Tory minister. Her sexual escapades with the high and mighty made the front-page news. The British media was quick to compare her to Christine Keeler, white showgirl and model, whose affairs with a Tory cabinet minister John Profumo and a Russian diplomat were seen as a "propah" sex scandal. That was 1963. Pamella Bordes, a former Miss India, was exposed in 1989. *News of the World* published the "Commons Call Girl" story featuring the researcher. Other newspapers jumped in. Noting the tone of their coverage of Pamella, the *Los Angeles Times* correspondent in London, reported: "British Sex Scandal—but 'It Ain't What It Used to Be'" That, at least, appears to be the verdict of connoisseurs of the genre who say they have been simultaneously riveted and slightly disappointed by reports dominating the nation's press for nearly two weeks on the social life of a former Miss India beauty queen, he wrote.

The woman, a parliamentary researcher, reputedly offered her nocturnal favors for the equivalent of $875 to a *News of the World* reporter posing as a wealthy Hong Kong businessman. A flurry of reports linked her with MPs, journalists, a government minister who escorted her to a Conservative Party ball and a Libyan intelligence official.

For added atmosphere, the story is unfolding against the backdrop of a titillating new film on the so-called Profumo affair, which helped topple a Conservative government 25 years ago. Called "Scandal," the box-office hit recalls the infamous affair between Britain's then-secretary of defense, John Profumo, and party girl Christine Keeler. But the adventures of India-born Pamella Bordes appear so far to fall well short of the mark set by the Profumo scandal.

"This extraordinary story has that mix of sex, security, sanctimoniousness and silliness which are essential to the great British scandal," the *Independent* newspaper noted in an editorial on the Bordes affair the other day. However, the paper added, "the tale does not, in point of seriousness, yet rank with the Keeler affair." "Ms. Bordes is, to be blunt, a bimbo," the newspaper declared. "There is something undignified about middle-aged men of influence, married or single, preening themselves so indiscreetly and so competitively in nightclubs or Conservative balls with such a lady." To date, the highest-ranking politician known to have escorted Bordes is Colin Moynihan, the unmarried minister for sport who took her to his party's winter ball.

It was asked how the parliamentary security system could have been so lax as to issue Bordes a pass allowing her access to the House of Commons without being searched. And there is considerable interest in how she came to live in a $1.3-million

Westminster penthouse equipped with a "division bell"—a device that informs members of Parliament a vote is about to be taken.

Even the tabloid *Daily Mail* couldn't resist a tongue-in-cheek comment on the difference 25 years has made. "Unless the delectable and dangerous Pamella Bordes turns out to have given the Libyans inside knowledge of possible amendments to the Football Spectators Bill," wrote columnist Keith Waterhouse, "I am afraid we are not in for a scandal of Profumo proportions." As a sequel to the Profumo affair, observes the *Economist* magazine, "the Bordes episode is still Hamlet without the prince."

Sunday Times columnist Simon Jenkins noted that the name of Miss Bordes is linked not to Soviet attaches but to editors, porn kings and Arab horse dealers: a case not so much for MI-5 as for the Health and Safety at Work Inspectorate. "These moments are precious in the dull history of the mother of parliaments," Jenkins added.

* * *

None of these liaisons led to Pamela's marriage. Personal Anglo-Indian encounters in India used to result in marriages.

BISHOP'S SON WED INDIAN

A N Anglican Bishop's son was married in India yesterday to a native girl, a Gond.

He is Mr. Verrier Elwin, son of Bishop Elwin, of Sierra
Leone, and former chaplain at Merton College, Oxford.

His wedding to Miss Koslarani was performed in accordance with
the Gond rites.

They will live in the Gond country, where Mr. Elwin's work has
earned him the name of the Indian St. Francis of Assisi.

Sex & British Empire

The scene in the British India has been described in the books recording personal histories. One is written by Jeremy Paxman— *Empire: What Ruling the World Did to the British.* "I now commenced a regular course of f——— with native women," writes Edward Sellon in one of the rare accounts of sexual relations in the early days of the Raj. In his memoirs he paints a picture of available young Indian women who "understood in perfection all the arts and wiles of love".

White Mughals by William Dalrymple

Very interesting material on this theme was unearthed by writer-historian William Dalrymple who detected a measure of multiculturalism in the secret and at times blatantly open British activity in India. Dalrymple's exploration became obsessive when he came across the extraordinary case of James Achilles Kirkpatrick, the British resident (in effect, ambassador) at the court of Hyderabad, had "connected himself with a female" of one of Hyderabad's leading noble families. The girl in question, Khair un-Nissa, was said to be little more than 14 years old at the time. Perhaps most alarmingly for the authorities in Bengal, it was said that Kirkpatrick had formally married the girl, which meant embracing Islam, and that he had become a practicing Shi'a Muslim. These rumours had led some of his colleagues to wonder whether his political loyalties could still be depended on. "I had been working in the India Office library on the papers of Kirkpatrick for several months before members of my own Scottish family started popping up in the story." William Dalrymple deals with this dimension of the Anglo-Indian encounter at length in his book *The White Mughals: Love & Betrayal in Eighteenth Century India.* "My relations suddenly became a lot more interesting, however, with the appearance in the story of a Muslim princess with the somewhat unexpected name of Mooti Begum Dalrymple, a woman whose name had certainly been rigorously removed from all the family records I had seen at home. Mooti turned out to be the daughter of the Nawab of the nearby port of Masulipatam and was married to James Dalrymple." Based on overwhelming evidence, Dalrymple draws the conclusion that the world inhabited by Sahib Begum/Kitty Kirkpatrick was far more hybrid, and had far less clearly defined ethnic, national and religious borders, than we have all been conditioned to expect. It is certainly unfamiliar to anyone who accepts at face value the usual rigid caricature of the Englishman in India, presented repeatedly in films and television dramas, of the imperialist incarnate: the narrow-minded sahib in a sola topee, dressing for dinner in the jungle while raising a disdainful nose at both the people and the culture of India. "As I progressed in my research, it was not long before I discovered that I had a direct Indian ancestor, was the product of a similar interracial liaison from this period and had Indian blood in my veins. No one in my family seemed to know about this, though it should not have been a surprise: we had all heard the stories of how our beautiful, dark-eyed, Calcutta-born great-great-grandmother, Sophia Pattle, with whom the painter Sir Edward Burne-Jones had fallen in love, used to speak Hindustani with her sisters and was painted by Frederick Watts with a *rakhi* - a Hindu sacred thread - tied around her wrist. But it was only when I poked around in the archives that discovered that she was descended from a Hindu Bengali woman from Chandernagore, who had converted to Catholicism, taken the name Marie Monica, and married a French officer." Dalrymple says: "I am sure that I am hardly alone in making this sort of discovery."

This history drives him to strike an optimistic note in this era of bigotry and rising hatred for the other. He writes in *The Guardian*: "The story of mixed-race families such as my own and the Kirkpatricks seems to raise huge questions about Britishness and the nature of empire, faith and personal identity; indeed, about how far all of these matter, are fixed and immutable - and to what extent they were flexible, tractable and negotiable."

"It is significant, moreover, that all this surprises us as much as it does: it is as if the Victorians succeeded in colonising not just India but also, more permanently, our imaginations, to the exclusion of all other images of the Indo-British encounter", writes Dalrymple.

THE PEERAGE

Mooti Begum1

F, #359335 Last Edited- 23 Aug 2009

Mooti Begum is the daughter of Nawab of Masulipatan. She married Lt.-Col. James Dalrymple, son of Sir William Dalrymple of Cousland, 3rd Bt. and Anne Philp. Her married name became Dalrymple.

Children of Mooti Begum and Lt.-Col. James Dalrymple

1. Noorjah Dalrymple

2. George Wemyss-Dalrymple+1 b. 1800,
d. 1 Jan 1848

MIXED MARRIAGES

Bibidom in British India

A tradition of the times when Hindus were not awake and never shouted "Love Jihad".

Innumerable cases of the mixed-race marriages have been recorded. Colonel James Skinner, founder of the Indian cavalry regiment Skinner's Horse, was the son of a Scottish officer and his Rajput mistress (though this was denied by many of his family).

Eighty children claimed him as their father. One of the great spectacles of early 19th-century Delhi was the sight of the East India Company resident, Sir David Ochterlony, taking the evening air by riding an elephant around the Red Fort, followed by his 13 Indian wives, each mounted on her own elephant.

Great pity, no opera based on this was staged during the celebrations of the UK-India Year of Culture in 2017.

Indian writer Pran Nevile did extensive work on this theme. Some extracts from his book *Beyond The Veil: Indian Women In The Raj:*

Many of the irregular unions of the sahibs with Bibis were considered respectable. There was no shame or stigma attached to these liaisons. Even the Governor General, Sir John Shore, and the Governor of Bombay and members of his Council, publicly had native women as their mistresses. These irregular unions attracted no censure.

***

The will of Henry Littleton, a company official, testifies to the virtues of his Bibi, a Brahmin woman, called Raja, whom he had willed all his property and possessions. Then we had the case of General John Pater who was so fond of his Bibi, that he built a church over her grave when the chaplain refused to bury her in the cemetery.

***

Dr. John Shortt, Company surgeon at Madras during the latter half of the 19th Century, was charmed by the grace and beauty of Telugu girls. He recorded, "I have seen several of these girls in my professional capacity, while they lived as mistresses with European officers, and have been greatly surprised at their ladylike manner, modesty and gentleness. Such beautiful small hands and little taper fingers, the ankles neatly turned, as to meet the admiration of the greatest connoisseur ... This is not to be wondered at that these girls are preferred to their own country women".

There was an army colonel who even consented to be circumcised to get possession of a beautiful Muslim woman who imposed this condition before becoming his Bibi.

***

It sounds amusing to find that an English Editor of a local paper advised sahibs in 1783, to sleep with Indian women to keep themselves cool in the beastly summer of Calcutta. In fact, the Portuguese obtained a firman from the Mughal emperor, Shahjahan, to keep Bengali women during summer to protect themselves from the heat of the Delta.

***

In the 1830s a magistrate in India had written home that he had "observed that those who have lived with a native woman for any length of time never marry a European... so amusingly playful, so anxious to oblige and please, that a person after being accustomed to their society shrinks from the idea of encountering the whims or yielding to the fancies of an Englishwoman".

***

Resorting to Bibis and mistresses was not only a piece of erotic expediency, but these, "sleeping dictionaries" helped the sahibs to learn about the lifestyle, customs and manners, besides languages, of India. The Bibi identified herself with the interests of her protector. She was an efficient housekeeper and a devoted nurse to her man when he fell ill.

*****

At times, their mutual love and respect was touching. The Bibi of a sahib was highly respected in society. Emma Roberts writes that "Indian women, Hindu or Muslim, when they are attached to Englishmen confine themselves with singular dignity to the *Zenana* of their protectors as if the marriage had taken place according to their own customs and ceremonies. They never go out of their houses and behave like a lawful wife of Muslim or Hindu of rank". The Bibikhana or "Ladyhouse" in a corner of the compound, separate from the main house, was an accepted feature of many a European bungalow.

*****

They were seldom a secret, as can be gathered from the account of the birth of Qui Hi's son, in the satiric poem:

The Grand Master

Poor Gulab was in that way,

That those who "love their lords" should be.

And in a week, to Qui Hi's joy,

Produced our youth a chopping boy.

Our hero now, without pretence,

Thought himself of some consequence.

A child he had got, and what was curious,

He knew the infant was not spurious.

For though Qui Hi was never tied

By licence to his Indian bride,

Yet he was confident that she

Had acted with fidelity.

***

The classic case is that of Job Charnock, founder of the city of Calcutta, who married a beautiful Brahmin girl, Leela, after rescuing her from a funeral pyre where she was going to perform "Sati". Legend has it that Charnock was madly in love with her and she persuaded the great sahib to live almost like a Hindu. We come across another case of romantic and perilous adventure of an English army officer who rescued a young and beautiful Brahmin widow at Rajamundary and took her in as his Bibi. Another illustrious company official, Francis Day, proved his deep attachment to his Bibi by choosing a site for the fort in Madras in 1639 which was close to her place.

Contemporary paintings depict the intimacy and closeness between the sahib and his Indian Bibi.

William Hickey, a famous attorney and socialite of Calcutta, in 1780-90's has left a touching account of his attachment to his Bibi, Jemdanee, which is as striking as the British artist, Thomas Hickey's aesthetic portrait of this charming and dignified lady. "Jemdanee", William Hickey wrote, "lived with me, respected and admired by all friends for her extraordinary sprightliness and great humour. Unlike the women in Asia, she never secluded herself from the sight of strangers; on the contrary, she delighted in joining my male parties, cordially joining in the mirth which prevailed though never touching wine or spirits of any kind". He extols her "as gentle and affectionately attached a girl, as ever man was blessed with". Jemdanee was a great favourite with Hickey's friends who gave her presents and sent her affectionate messages. Two of them, Bob Pott and Col. Cooper, also had faithful Bibis.

***

Another distinguished sahib with Indian Bibis was General William Palmer, who lived with an aristocratic Muslim lady, Begum Faiz Bakhsh, a member of the Delhi royal house, and a second Bibi, a princess of Oudh. In his will, Palmer bequeathed his house to her and referred to her as "Bibi Faiz Bakhsh Saheba who has been my affectionate friend and companion during a period of more than 35 years (1781-1816)".

Richard Burton wrote in his autobiography that Indian mistresses were a regular feature of British military life. In 1840, there was hardly an officer in Baroda, who was not more or less, tied to a Hindu woman. In many cases the mistresses followed the regiment and lived with their protectors for many years and bore children to them.

However, mostly these irregular unions were temporary under an agreement and ceased when the regiment left the station. Bibis and mistresses were left behind when the sahibs returned home. It was a moving sight when they stood with their children on the riverbank bidding farewell to their protectors as the vessel bore them away. The pathos of such a parting finds expression in a contemporary ballad sung by an Indian woman:

Tis thy will and I must leave thee,

O thou best beloved farewell

I forbear lest I should grieve thee,

Half my heart felt pangs to tell.

Soon a British fair will charm thee,

Thou alas her smiles must woo,

But tho 'she to rapture warm thee.

Don't forget thy poor Hindoo.

The Bibidom did not last, thanks to the introduction of the steamships that brought English wives and husband-hunting women to Indian shores. The Memsahibs launched a powerful campaign against their Oriental rivals. The Indian Mutiny helped their cause. Thus, marrying beyond the pale and intermingling without marrying almost ended.

———